Group's

hands·On BiBLE curriculum ™

Grades 5 and 6
Winter

Teacher Guide

WHEN JESUS CAME
RELATIONSHIPS
MONEY AND TIME

Group
Loveland, Colorado

Group

Hands-On Bible Curriculum™, Grades 5 and 6, Winter
Copyright © 1992, 1994, 1996, and 1998 Group Publishing, Inc.

First Printing, 1998 Edition

Credits

Contributing Authors: Patti Chromey, Nancy Dunn, Mikal Keefer, Karl and Gina Leuthauser,
    Steve and Annie Wamberg, Michael D. Warden, and Paul Woods
Editor: Jim Hawley
Senior Editors: Ivy Beckwith and Paul Woods
Chief Creative Officer: Joani Schultz
Copy Editors: Julie Meiklejohn and Patti Leach
Art Director: Kari K. Monson
Designer: Dori Walker
Cover Art Director: Janet Barker
Cover Designers: Janet Barker and Helen H. Lannis
Cover Photographer: Tim O'Hara
Computer Graphic Artist: Joyce Douglas
Illustrators: Jeff Carnehl and Ray Tollison
Audio Engineer: Steve Saavedra
Production Manager: Peggy Naylor

ISBN 0-7644-0107-6
Printed in the United States of America.

CONTENTS

MinistryNet

To help make your teaching more effective, Group is providing MinistryNet™, our free online service. With this service, you'll get:

- Helpful teacher ideas for each week's lesson.
- Access to a message board with other teachers of Hands-On Bible Curriculum™.
- Plus, all the other timesaving MinistryNet helps for your children's and youth ministries.

In order to use this service, you'll need your own Internet access plus a World Wide Web browser that supports Java™ script and applets. We recommend the newest version of Microsoft Internet Explorer or Netscape Navigator. You can download these browsers from their websites if you do not already have one installed.

Once you have the necessary items above, use your browser to connect to Group Publishing's website at http://www.grouppublishing.com. You can then click on the button for MinistryNet and look for a button that will allow you to set up your free Hands-On Bible Curriculum service.

Then log into MinistryNet and begin to connect with other Hands-On Bible Curriculum teachers and get timely Teacher Tips for your lessons.

MEETING THE REAL NEEDS OF PRETEENS

Fifth- and sixth-graders are in transition between their elementary years and teen years. They are more sophisticated than the seventh graders of just a few years ago, yet they are still children in many ways. They want purposeful learning, but they want to have fun while learning. Most sixth graders and even some fifth graders enter middle school and experience pressures that didn't exist for them in elementary school. Kids are faced with more choices, responsibilities, and temptations. Alcohol, drugs, sexuality, gangs, violence, family problems, school struggles, and friendship issues all confront kids at this age.

These preteen kids provide an opportunity to develop curriculum that will be both fun and sophisticated. After listening to teachers and kids themselves, we have overhauled our Hands-On Bible Curriculum™ for fifth- and sixth-graders.

The lessons are still active and fun, but now they challenge kids with more sophisticated activities that develop kids' emerging higher-level thinking skills. Kids are encouraged to discover the "why" behind what they are learning. In addition, many new, age-appropriate Learning Lab gizmos have been selected, and all gizmos are now more significant to the lessons' activities.

TEACHING AS JESUS TAUGHT

People may think active learning is new. Actually, active learning was used nearly 2,000 years ago by the master teacher, Jesus.

Think back to a major life lesson you've learned. Did you learn it from reading about it? from hearing about it? or from something you did? Most likely you learned your life lesson from something you experienced.

When Jesus taught people he actively involved them in the learning process. The disciples learned a powerful lesson when they experienced the impact of Jesus' feeding of the 5,000 and gathered up the leftovers.

That's what active learning is—learning by doing. Here are kids' basic learning needs that active learning fulfills:

1. KIDS NEED ACTION

Aircraft pilots know well the difference between passive and active learning. Their passive learning comes through listening to flight instructors and reading flight-instruction books. Their active learning comes through actually flying an airplane or flight simulator. Books and lectures may be helpful, but pilots really learn to fly by manipulating a plane's controls themselves.

In a similar way, Jesus trained his followers, teaching and demonstrating what he wanted them to learn. But their real learning came when Jesus sent out the seventy-two followers and let them learn through hands-on experience (Luke 10).

We can help young people learn through active learning, too. Though we may engage students passively in some reading and listening to teachers, their understanding and application of God's Word will really take off through simulated and real-life experiences.

Forms of active learning include simulation games, role-plays, service projects, experiments, group pantomimes, construction projects, purposeful games, field trips, and, of course, the most powerful form of active learning of all—real-life experiences.

We can more fully explain active learning by exploring four of its characteristics:

◆ **Active learning is an adventure.** Passive learning is almost always predictable. Students sit passively while the teacher or speaker follows a planned outline or script.

In active learning, kids may learn lessons the teacher never envisioned. Because the leader trusts students to help create the learning experience, learners may venture into unforeseen discoveries. And often the teacher learns as much as the students.

◆ **Active learning is fun and captivating.** What are we communicating when we say, "OK, the fun's over—time to talk about God"? What's the hidden message? That joy is separate from God? And that learning is separate from joy?

Active learning is not joyless. One student we interviewed

clearly remembered her best Sunday school lesson: "Jesus was the light, and we went into a dark room and shut off the lights. We had a candle, and we learned that Jesus is the light and the dark can't shut off the light." That's active learning. Deena enjoyed the lesson. She had fun. And she learned.

◆ **Active learning involves everyone.** Here the difference between passive and active learning becomes abundantly clear. It's like the difference between watching a football game on television and actually playing in the game.

The "trust walk" provides a good example of involving everyone in active learning. Half of the group members put on blindfolds; the other half serve as guides. The "blind" people trust the guides to lead them through the building or outdoors. The guides prevent the blind people from falling down stairs or tripping over rocks. Everyone needs to participate to learn the inherent lessons of trust, faith, doubt, fear, confidence, and servanthood. Passive spectators of this experience would learn little, but participants learn a great deal.

◆ **Active learning is focused through debriefing.** Activity simply for activity's sake doesn't usually result in good learning. Debriefing—evaluating an experience by discussing it in pairs or small groups—helps focus the experience and draw out its meaning. Debriefing helps sort and order the information students gather during the experience. It helps learners relate the recently experienced activity to their lives.

The process of debriefing is best started immediately after an experience. We generally use a three-step process in debriefing: reflection, interpretation, and application.

Reflection—This first step asks the students, "How did you feel?" Active-learning experiences typically evoke an emotional reaction, so it's appropriate to begin debriefing at that level.

When you're debriefing, use open-ended questions to probe feelings. Avoid questions that can be answered with "yes" or "no." Let your learners know that there are no wrong answers to these "feeling" questions.

Interpretation—The next step in the debriefing process asks: "What does this mean to you? How is this experience like or unlike some other aspect of your life?" Now you're asking people to identify a message or principle from the experience.

You want your learners to discover the message for themselves. So instead of telling students your answers, take the time to ask questions that encourage discovery. Use Scripture and discussion in pairs or small groups to explore how the actions and effects of the activity might translate to kids' lives.

Application—The final debriefing step asks, "What will you do about it?" This step moves learning into action. Your young people have shared a common experience. They've discovered a principle. Now they must create something new with what they've just experienced and interpreted. They must integrate the message into their lives.

The application stage of debriefing calls for a decision. Ask your students how they'll change, how they'll grow, and what they'll do as a result of your time together.

2. KIDS NEED TO THINK

After Jesus washed the disciples' feet, he asked, "Do you understand what I have done for you?" Jesus challenged the disciples to think about his example of servanthood.

Today's students have been trained not to think. They aren't dumber than previous generations. We've simply conditioned them not to use their heads.

You see, we've trained our kids to respond with the simplistic answers they think the teacher wants to hear. We give kids fill-in-the-blank student workbooks with word scrambles and missing-letter puzzles. Teachers ask dead-end questions such as "What's the capital of Delaware?" Such fact-recall methods have produced kids and adults who have learned not to think.

Helping kids think requires a paradigm shift in how we teach. We need to plan for and set aside time for higher-order thinking and be willing to reduce our time spent on lower-order parroting. Group's Hands-On Bible Curriculum is designed to help you do just that.

Thinking classrooms look quite different from traditional classrooms. In many church environments, the teacher does most of the talking and hopes that knowledge will somehow transmit from his or her brain to the students'. In thinking settings, the teacher coaches students to ponder, wonder, imagine, and problem-solve.

3. KIDS NEED TO TALK

Everyone knows that the person who learns the most in any class is the teacher. Explaining a concept to someone else is usually more helpful to the explainer than to the listener. So why not let the students do more teaching? That's one of the chief benefits of letting kids do the talking. This process is called interactive learning.

What is interactive learning? Interactive learning occurs

when students discuss and work cooperatively in pairs or small groups. It honors the fact that students can learn from one another, not just from the teacher. Students work together in pairs or small groups to accomplish shared goals. They build together, discuss together, and present together. They teach each other and learn from one another. Success as a group is celebrated. Positive interdependence promotes individual and group learning.

Jesus used interactive learning with the twelve disciples. He sent them out together as a group. When arguments arose over who was the greatest in the group, Jesus helped the disciples recognize they were not competing against one another. He turned their interaction into a learning experience.

Here's a selection of interactive learning techniques that are used in Group's Hands-On Bible Curriculum. With any of these examples, leaders may assign students to specific partners or small groups. This will maximize cooperation and learning by preventing all the "rowdies" from linking up. And it will allow for new friendships to form outside of established cliques.

Pair-Share—With this technique each student turns to a partner and responds to a question or problem from the teacher or leader. Every learner responds. There are no passive observers. The teacher may then ask students to share their partners' responses.

Study Partners—Most curricula and most teachers call for Scripture passages to be read to the whole class by one person. One reads; the others doze.

Why not relinquish some teacher control and let partners read and react with each other? They'll all be involved—and will learn more.

Learning Groups—Students work together in small groups to create a model, design artwork, or study a passage or story; then they discuss what they learned through the experience. Each person in the learning group may be assigned a specific role. Here are some examples:

> **Reader,**
> **Recorder** (makes notes of key thoughts expressed during the reading or discussion),
> **Reporter** (reports to the class the answers arrived at by the group), and
> **Encourager** (urges silent members to share their thoughts).

When everyone has a specific responsibility, knows what it is, and contributes to a small group, much is accomplished and much is learned.

Jigsaw—Each person in a small group examines a different concept, Scripture, or part of an issue. Then each person teaches the others in the group. Thus, all members teach and all must learn the others' discoveries. This technique is called a jigsaw because individuals are responsible to their group for different pieces of the puzzle.

Following any period of partner or small-group work, the leader may reconvene the entire class for large-group processing. During this time the teacher may ask for reports or discoveries from individuals or teams. This technique builds in accountability for the teacherless pairs and small groups.

YOU CAN DO IT, TOO!

Group's Hands-On Bible Curriculum makes it easy for you to use active and interactive learning with your group. Using the gizmos and gadgets in the Learning Lab, Bibles, and some common classroom supplies, you can make learning fun and help your kids' faith grow.

For more information on incorporating active and interactive learning into your teaching, check out *Why Nobody Learns Much of Anything at Church: And How to Fix It* by Thom and Joani Schultz (Group Publishing).

HELPFUL TIPS FOR TEACHERS

Now that you know why and how active and interactive learning will make a significant impact on your kids' lives, here are some tips to make active learning work best for you:

◆ Read through the whole lesson before class. Try out the lessons' gizmos in the Learning Lab. Note Teacher Tips in the margin to alert you to specific helps for an activity.

◆ Recognize the difference between good "learning noise" and a situation needing your attention. Active-learning activities often are fast-paced and noisy—which is good. After the experience, you signal the kids to begin to reflect and process the activity.

◆ Be creative with your learning space. Move tables aside so kids can move around freely and work in groups. Look for other areas in your church that could be used for activities, such as a foyer, a parking lot, or a fellowship hall.

◆ Remember with active learning everyone is a participant—so join in the learning with your kids!

◆ Look for teachable moments. An activity that bombs may provide a wonderful opportunity for learning if you ask

---

COMMON CLASSROOM SUPPLIES

- ◆ Bible reference materials
- ◆ candles
- ◆ cassette player
- ◆ chalkboard and chalk
- ◆ dictionaries
- ◆ glue or glue stick
- ◆ index cards
- ◆ markers
- ◆ masking tape
- ◆ matches
- ◆ newsprint
- ◆ old magazines
- ◆ old newspapers
- ◆ paper clips
- ◆ pencils
- ◆ scissors
- ◆ snacks
- ◆ stapler
- ◆ transparent tape
- ◆ trash cans

questions such as "Why didn't this work out?" "How is this like what happens in real life?" or "What can we learn from this experience?"

◆ Remember that kids learn in different ways. The activities in each lesson are designed to reach the different learning styles of your students. Don't shy away from an unfamiliar activity—you may even find that one activity helps you learn even more than the student who needed it most.

◆ Get to know your kids. Use a fun question such as "If you were an animal, what would you be and why?" or choose an affirmation game from the Bonus Ideas. Make kids feel welcome at the beginning of each class period. Call your kids by name. Use name tags if needed. Your sincere interest in each student will greatly enhance the experiences you'll share with them.

◆ Adapt the lessons to fit your class. Simply choose activities that will work best for your kids. Since The Point is made in each activity, you'll have taught something significant even if you don't get through the whole lesson. Use the Bonus Ideas beginning on page 139 or the Time Stuffers found in the module introductions to lengthen a lesson, if needed.

◆ Remember to photocopy the "Table Talk" handout to give to kids after each lesson. If available, use colored paper to add variety. Encourage kids to use the Table Talk with their families.

◆ Don't show kids the contents of the Learning Lab before the lessons they are used in. This will keep kids' interest high.

◆ Make your class a "safe zone" for kids with special needs and learning disabilities. Avoid calling on kids to read or pray if they find it embarrassing. Talk to the parents of kids with disabilities to find out how best to help them.

Assure students that *all* Christians are part of the body of Christ, each with special talents and gifts he or she can use to serve him.

◆ Use the learning activities to draw out the strengths of your students. While in small-group activity, a student who doesn't read well could be a reporter or encourager.

◆ Be aware of the attitudes kids bring into class. Some kids may walk in after a family fight or a disappointing experience at school. Encourage kids to share their feelings. Then be patient as they work to overcome their bad days.

UNDERSTANDING YOUR FIFTH- AND SIXTH-GRADERS

MENTAL DEVELOPMENT

- Have well-developed critical-thinking and problem-solving skills.
- Are beginning to question authority figures; prefer to reason things through for themselves.
- Are interested in how past and present world events affect their lives.

SOCIAL DEVELOPMENT

- Spend a lot of time with one best friend.
- Usually prefer to stick to same-sex friendships but may also begin to explore boyfriend-girlfriend relationships.
- Thrive on organized games and group activities.

EMOTIONAL DEVELOPMENT

- Frequently get mixed messages about being children or being mature and ready to accept responsibility for choices and actions.
- Are subject to strong fears about losing parents, being abandoned, being rejected by friends, being victims of violence, or becoming ill.
- Are strongly influenced by heroes and role models.

PHYSICAL DEVELOPMENT

- Have high energy levels and demand a lot of physical activity.
- Girls tend to be taller and more physically developed than boys.
- Boys often find this intimidating and tend to avoid physical contact with girls.

SPIRITUAL DEVELOPMENT

- Want everything to be fair.
- Want to test what they've been taught about God against their own experiences.
- Are able to make choices about finding God's will and following it.

Dear Parent,

I'm so glad to be your child's teacher this quarter. With our Hands-On Bible Curriculum™, your preteen will look at Bible study in a whole new way.

For the next thirteen weeks, we'll explore what Scripture has to say to fifth- and sixth-graders about when Jesus came, relationships, and money and time. Using active-learning methods and a surprising assortment of gadgets and gizmos (such as "prism scopes" and "pumice rocks"), we'll help kids discover meaningful applications of God's Word.

Our Hands-On Bible Curriculum welcomes you to play an important part in what your child learns. **Each week kids will receive a "Table Talk" handout to take home and share.** The "Table Talk" contains a thought-provoking story with a Scripture and discussion-starters and family-building ideas—all focused on The Point of our Bible lesson for the week.

Let me encourage you to use the "Table Talk" regularly; it's a great tool for reinforcing Bible truths and promoting positive, healthy communication in your family.

Sincerely,

WHEN JESUS CAME

The birth of Jesus Christ is one of the Bible's most loved stories.

Usually, kids learn the story at a very young age. And by the time kids reach elementary age, they not only spout the proper words, but they often do so with little emotion. In other words, one of God's greatest miracles is often reduced to mere "Sunday school" answers.

But the story of Jesus' birth is more than a collection of words for the season of Christmas. On the contrary, the Incarnation is foundational to Christianity. God becoming man. Divinity taking on flesh and blood. Faith in Christ's birth is but the beginning of understanding the entire gospel message.

Developing an active faith must become a high priority for young people today, especially preteens. These four lessons will do more than just retell a familiar story to kids; they'll also reveal the importance of faithfulness and obedience in the lives of God's people.

"O come, all ye faithful…O come, let us adore him!"

FOUR LESSONS ON WHEN JESUS CAME

LESSON	PAGE	THE POINT	THE BIBLE BASIS
1—Ready and Waiting	15	People who truly love God obey him faithfully.	Luke 1:26-38
2—John's Message	24	We can prepare for Jesus' coming.	Luke 3:2b-4
3—Celebrating Jesus' Birth	34	Jesus' birth is something to celebrate!	Luke 2:1-20
4—Jesus, Our Example	44	Becoming like Jesus means caring about others.	Philippians 2:1-11

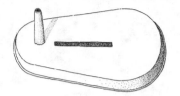

THE SIGNAL

During the lessons on when Jesus came, your signal to get kids back together during activities will be to sound the *noisemaker* found in the Learning Lab. In response to sounding the *noisemaker,* have kids stop what they're doing and focus on you for their next instructions.

Tell kids about this signal before the lesson begins. Explain that it's important to respond to this signal quickly so the class can do as many fun activities as possible.

THE TIME STUFFER

This module's Time Stuffer will encourage kids to remember The Point of each lesson throughout the week. There are sentence starters that correspond to each week's lesson next to the balloon bouquets on the "Celebration Bouquets" poster found in the Learning Lab.

During their free moments, kids can choose a sentence starter and write a sentence completion in one of the balloons. At the end of this module, you'll have a poster full of ideas about how to celebrate Jesus' coming.

REMEMBERING THE BIBLE

Each four- or five-week module focuses on a Key Bible Verse. The Key Verse for this module is "For this reason Christ is the mediator of a new covenant, that those who are called may receive the promised eternal inheritance" **(Hebrews 9:15a).**

Look for the Key Verse Connection in the margin of each lesson to tie the Key Verse to The Point of the lesson.

READY AND WAITING

THE POINT

People who truly love God obey him faithfully.

THE BIBLE BASIS

Luke 1:26-38

In the sixth month, God sent the angel Gabriel to Nazareth, a town in Galilee, to a virgin pledged to be married to a man named Joseph, a descendant of David. The virgin's name was Mary. The angel went to her and said, "Greetings, you who are highly favored! The Lord is with you."

Mary was greatly troubled at his words and wondered what kind of greeting this might be. But the angel said to her, "Do not be afraid, Mary, you have found favor with God. You will be with child and give birth to a son, and you are to give him the name Jesus. He will be great and will be called the Son of the Most High. The Lord God will give him the throne of his father David, and he will reign over the house of Jacob forever; his kingdom will never end."

"How will this be," Mary asked the angel, "since I am a virgin?"

The angel answered, "The Holy Spirit will come upon you, and the power of the Most High will overshadow you. So the holy one to be born will be called the Son of God. Even Elizabeth your relative is going to have a child in her old age, and she who was said to be barren is in her six month. For nothing is impossible with God."

"I am the Lord's servant," Mary answered. "May it be to me as you have said." Then the angel left her.

KEY VERSE

for Lessons 1–4

"For this reason Christ is the mediator of a new covenant, that those who are called may receive the promised eternal inheritance."

(Hebrews 9:15a)

A visitor from another realm tells a young, innocent girl that she's been chosen to be the mother of a son who will save the world. It sounds like a plot from a fantasy novel. Yet, when Mary heard the angel's message, she humbly believed it and obeyed without hesitation.

Today's kids long for the time when they will be in control of what they do and where they go. It may be hard for them to see obedience to God as a good thing. But your fifth- and sixth-graders can learn that obedience to God will help them to live fulfilling lives. Mary was likely a young teen, not a lot older than today's sixth-graders, when she responded in obedience to God. Use this lesson to teach that faithful obedience springs from love and respect and that the rewards for obedience are well worth the effort.

Another Scripture used in this lesson is **Luke 1:39-49.**

GETTING THE POINT

Students will

◆ discover that obeying God means taking risks in faith,

◆ learn that God faithfully rewards obedience, and

◆ encourage one another's obedience to God.

THIS LESSON AT A GLANCE

Before the lesson, collect the necessary items from the Learning Lab for the activities you plan to use. Refer to the pictures in the margin to see what each item looks like.

SECTION	MINUTES	WHAT STUDENTS WILL DO	LEARNING LAB SUPPLIES	CLASSROOM SUPPLIES
ATTENTION GRABBER	up to 10	**The Waiting Game**—Listen and wait for their names to be called.	Two-tone superball	
BIBLE EXPLORATION AND APPLICATION	up to 15	**Love Worth Taking Risks For**—Determine what risks they'd take for people they love, and explore Luke 1:26-38.	Noisemaker	Bibles, paper, scissors, pencils, "Way to Obey!" handouts (p. 22)
	up to 14	**Friends to Help Me Obey**—Using plastic rings, recall the good things God gives when they obey him, and discuss Luke 1:39-45.	Plastic rings, neon shoelaces	Bible
	up to 13	**Obedience Song**—Read Mary's song in Luke 1:46-49 before writing lyrics praising God for times they're obedient to him.		Bibles, paper, pencils or pens
CLOSING	up to 8	**Sticking Together**—Commit to helping each other obey God.	Sticky sports ball	

Remember to make photocopies of the "Table Talk" handout (p. 23) to send home with your kids. "Table Talk" is a valuable tool for helping fifth- and sixth-graders talk with their parents about what they're learning in class.

THE LESSON

As kids arrive, teach them the signal for the quarter. Tell kids that whenever you sound the *noisemaker,* they're to stop what they're doing and look at you without talking. Explain that when you have everyone's attention, you'll continue the lesson.

TEACHER TIP

It's important to say The Point as it's written in each activity. Repeating The Point over and over throughout the lesson will help kids remember it and apply it to their lives.

ATTENTION GRABBER

THE WAITING GAME

(up to 10 minutes)

Have kids stand in a circle, facing outward. Stand in the center of the circle, holding the *two-tone superball* found in the Learning Lab. Say: **When your name is called, quickly turn around and catch the item I'll be throwing to you. Don't turn around unless your name is called.**

Call a student's name, and throw the *two-tone superball* to him or her. When the student catches the ball (or retrieves it if it gets away), have him or her call another student's name and toss the ball to that person. Play until each student's name has been called. Don't worry if students don't catch the ball.

Collect the *two-tone superball* for use in later activities.

Have kids turn around and sit down. Ask:

◆ **What were you thinking when your name was called?**

◆ **How is that like the way you feel when you realize God wants you to do something?**

◆ **What was it like to catch or drop the ball?**

◆ **How is that like how you feel when you obey or disobey God?**

Say: **It's not easy to always be ready to obey God. But it feels great when we do obey God. When we don't obey, it's easy to feel that we've "dropped the ball."**  **People who truly love God obey him faithfully. So we need to be ready to hear and obey what God wants us to do.**

LEARNING LAB

◆ THE **POINT**

LEARNING LAB

▬KEY VERSE
CONNECTION

"For this reason Christ is the mediator of a new covenant, that those who are called may receive the promised eternal inheritance" (Hebrews 9:15a).

Fifth- and sixth-graders are used to rules. They see them as impositions and barriers. Use the Key Verse to show that as Christians, we obey God because we want to, not because we have to. Because of the new covenant with God that Jesus brings, we can express our love for God and our desire to grow closer to him by following his guidelines.

TEACHER TIP

If you have any groups with fewer than four kids, combine some of the roles within the group. For example, the scribe can also be the reporter. If you have groups larger than four, have kids in these groups rotate roles for each question.

LOVE WORTH TAKING RISKS FOR

(up to 15 minutes)

Hand out slips of paper and pencils. Have kids each write down the names of three or four people they love. These people could be family members, friends, teachers, someone from church, or another important person. Say: **Imagine one of the people you listed is in one of the following situations. Stand if you would take the risk, and stay seated if you wouldn't.**

Read the following situations:

◆ **As you're walking to school, you see the person you love in a car that's stalled on the train tracks. The latch on the seat belt is stuck, and the person can't get out. You can hear a train in the distance. Do you risk your life to try to save the person?**

◆ **You're just feeling accepted into a group of popular kids at your school. When you're walking down the hall with them, you see your best friend trip and scatter books all over the place. Your new friends insult your best friend with cruel words. Do you risk embarrassment and rejection from the group by going to help your best friend?**

◆ **One of your friends has started a friendship with a new kid who is kind of wild. One day you see this kid give drugs to your friend. Do you risk your friendship by talking to your friend or reporting what you saw to a teacher?**

After kids have responded to each situation, ask:

◆ **Was it easy or hard making your decisions? Why?**

◆ **How does the decision change when it's for someone you love?**

Have kids form groups of four. Give each group a Bible, a "Way to Obey!" handout (p. 22), and a pencil. Have each group appoint a reader to read the Bible passages and ask the questions, a scribe to write down the group's answers, an encourager to make sure everyone participates, and a reporter to tell the class about the group's discoveries. Tell kids you'll briefly sound the *noisemaker* every two minutes to let them know they should move along to the next question.

When groups have finished discussing the questions on their handouts, ask reporters to share their groups' answers with the whole class. Ask:

◆ **How was Mary's situation similar to the choices you made earlier with the people you loved? different?**

Say: **When Mary decided to obey God, it meant she would have a baby when she wasn't married. Other people may have gossiped about her or laughed at her, but she obeyed God anyway.** Ask:

◆ **How do people's reactions affect your willingness to obey God?**

◆ **What reaction from others makes it most difficult for you to obey God?**

Say: **Even when it's hard, people who truly love God obey him faithfully. Let's look at how we can be encouraged to obey God.**

BIBLE *INSIGHT*

Mary did not respond to the angel's message with disbelief, but simply with puzzlement. "How will this be?" she asked the angel. When the angel explained, she humbly accepted her role in God's unfolding plan. She must have known, though, that she would face embarrassment and suspicion because of her situation.

THE POINT

FRIENDS TO HELP ME OBEY

(up to 14 minutes)

You'll need to prepare for this activity before class. Tie the four *neon shoelaces* together, forming one long string. Count out a quantity of *plastic rings* equal to about three times the number of students in your class, and string them on the *neon shoelaces* (there are about 160 rings in the bag). Tie the two remaining ends of the *neon shoelaces* together, forming a large loop holding the *plastic rings*.

Hold up the *neon shoelace* loop and say: **This *neon shoelace* loop represents how friends have helped us be faithful to God.**

Share one example of how a friend encouraged you to be faithful, then slip your little finger inside one of the *plastic rings* (or simply grab one of the rings if your finger won't fit). Say: **Think about a time a friend has encouraged you to be faithful to God. When you have one example, come up to the *neon shoelace* loop and tell about the experience. You don't have to go into details if you don't want to. Then place your finger in one of the *plastic rings*, and pull the loop taut. Space yourselves around the loop, so everyone can fit around it. Be sure to leave at least two empty rings between your finger and your neighbors'.**

After everyone has joined the loop, say: **There are extra rings in our loop. Think up another one or two situations where friends have helped you be faithful. For**

LEARNING LAB

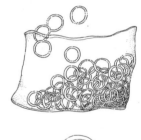

TEACHER TIP

Encourage active participation in the discussion by following up kids' answers with questions such as "What did you mean by that?" and "Can you tell me more?"

each situation you remember, place another finger in another *plastic ring*. There are enough rings for each person to have three rings.

Give kids a few minutes to recall examples and to put on the rings. Then ask:

◆ **What was it like to recall times your friends encouraged you?**

◆ **How is the way the *neon shoelaces* hold us all together like how your friends encourage you to obey God?**

Read **Luke 1:39-45** aloud. Ask:

◆ **How do you think Elizabeth's encouragement helped Mary to be faithful?**

◆ **How can your friends' encouragement help you obey God faithfully?**

 THE **POINT**

Say: **Just as Elizabeth encouraged Mary's obedience, we can encourage one another.** **People who truly love God obey him faithfully. Let's look at the blessings of that obedience.**

Return the *plastic rings* and *neon shoelaces* to the Learning Lab. Remember to untie the *neon shoelaces* before the next lesson.

OBEDIENCE SONG

(up to 13 minutes)

Give each student a Bible, paper, and a pencil or pen. Have a volunteer read **Luke 1:46-49** while the others follow along. Then say: **Mary obeyed God with such joy in her heart that she praised God with a song. Think about a time your obedience to God brought you joy. Then create two or three verses for a song that praises God for helping you to be obedient. Be sure to include how you were blessed for your obedience. Refer to Mary's song in Luke 1:46-49 if needed.**

Give kids about five minutes to create their songs. After five minutes ask:

◆ **What was it like writing a song praising God?**

Ask for volunteers to read their song lyrics to the class. Then ask:

◆ **How could this activity help you obey God more faithfully?**

 THE **POINT**

Say: **Praising God is one way that** **people who truly love God obey him faithfully. Let's encourage each other to obey God now.**

TABLE TALK

Christian education extends beyond the classroom into the home. Photocopy the "Table Talk" handout (p. 23) for this week, and send it home with your kids. Encourage kids and parents to use the handout to spark meaningful discussion on this week's topic. Follow up next week by asking kids how their discussions with their families went.

CLOSING

STICKING TOGETHER

(up to 8 minutes)

Form a circle. Ask:

◆ **What can you do to help one another obey God?**

Show kids the *sticky sports ball*. Hold the ball in your palm, and give the student next to you a "sticky" high five. Think of one way you can encourage him or her to obey God, such as saying, "I'll pray for you." Then say: **I'll stick by you by praying for you.** Then have that student think up a way to encourage the next person in the circle and say to him or her, "I'll stick by you by…" and give him or her a sticky high five with the *sticky sports ball*. Continue around the circle until everyone has been encouraged and you have the *sticky sports ball* again. Hold the ball up and say: **We've encouraged each other to stick together to help us be  people who truly love God and obey him faithfully.**

Return the *sticky sports ball* to your Learning Lab for use in later lessons.

LEARNING LAB

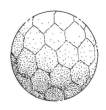

THE POINT

Way to Obey!

In your group, read Luke 1:26-38, and discuss these questions:

Question 1:

What risks did Mary take when she obeyed God? Was obeying God worth the risks? Why or why not?

Question 3:

If Mary hadn't loved God, would she have obeyed him? Why or why not? Is it easier to obey someone you love? Why or why not?

Question 2:

Why did Mary obey God? Why do you obey God?

Question 4:

What risks do you have to take to obey God? Is obeying God worth the risks? Why or why not?

Discussion Starters

- Why do you obey God?
- Talk about a time you were obedient to God when you didn't want to be or when you were afraid to be. Why did you choose to obey?
- What is the best motivation for obeying God?

Family Building

*For Kids Only: Ask God to show you areas in your life where you are being disobedient. Then ask God to forgive you and to help you change your behavior.

*For Parents Only: Ask the Holy Spirit to show you your sin. Be sensitive to unintentional sins as well. Seek forgiveness for your sins, and ask God for the grace to help you to make right choices in every circumstance.

*For the Family: Make a list that demonstrates why you would want to obey God. Start with looking at who God is. For example, you may want to obey God because he is kind. Expand your list by adding the benefits that come from obedience. For example, if we obey God, we won't hurt those we love.

Something to Think About

During America's slave-trading times, African tribesmen would hide in the territory of another tribe and wait for a child playing alone. The tribesmen would grab the child, tie his or her hands and feet, fling him or her over a shoulder, and take him or her to where the slave trader waited. A healthy child might bring the tribesmen ten dollars worth of cloth or beads. Often, the kidnappers were also chained and taken away by the slave traders.

On the plantations in America, slaves were often awakened at four o'clock in the morning. The last slave out of the quarters was whipped. They'd work sixteen to eighteen hours a day, seven days a week.

Slavery happened during one of the darkest times in American history. Men, women, and children were forced to obey their masters out of fear of punishment, torture, and death. The slaves usually obeyed—with a deep hatred and resentment for and fear of their masters.

How fortunate we are that the obedience God wants from us is nothing like the obedience the slave owners forced. The obedience God desires is based on our thankfulness and God's genuine love. Even if we chose to disobey, God continues to love us. Sometimes we face the consequences of bad choices. Sometimes God disciplines us like a loving parent. But God doesn't force us to obey. When we obey God, we find peace. That is exactly what God wants for us, but he doesn't *make us chose it.*

"I have set before you life and death, blessings and curses. Now choose life, so that you and your children may live and that you may love the Lord your God, listen to his voice, and hold fast to him"

(Deuteronomy 30:19b-20a).

Table Talk

Group's hands·On BiBLE curriculum

Ready and Waiting, Week 1

Permission to photocopy this handout from Group's Hands-On Bible Curriculum™ for Grades 5 and 6 granted for local church use. Copyright © Group Publishing, Inc., P.O. Box 481, Loveland, CO 80539.

JOHN'S MESSAGE

THE POINT

☞ **We can prepare for Jesus' coming.**

KEY *VERSE*
for Lessons 1–4

"For this reason Christ is the mediator of a new covenant, that those who are called may receive the promised eternal inheritance."

(Hebrews 9:15a)

THE BIBLE BASIS

Luke 3:2b-4

> The word of God came to John son of Zechariah in the desert.
> He went into all the country around the Jordan, preaching a baptism of repentance for the forgiveness of sins. As is written in the book of the words of Isaiah the prophet: "A voice of one calling in the desert, 'Prepare the way for the Lord, make straight paths for him.' "

John the Baptist's desert lifestyle, rough clothing, and confrontational message made him a real standout. His outspoken call to repentance drew the attention of those who were sincerely seeking God's will and the wrath of the rigidly legalistic religious leaders. John's faithfulness to God's message eventually cost him his life. But it also gave him the most honored supporting role in history as the one who prepared the way for the coming of Christ.

The very last thing most fifth- and sixth-graders want to do is stand out from the crowd. They find great security in conformity and anonymity. When we encourage kids to adopt a Christian lifestyle that will set them apart from their peers, we're asking them to do something that's difficult and scary. This lesson will help kids learn that they can prepare the way, as John did, for God to work in their own lives and in the lives of others.

Other Scriptures used in this lesson are **Matthew 3:1-6; Luke 3:3-6; John 13:34-35; 2 Corinthians 9:11-14; Philippians 2:12-16;** and **1 Peter 2:11-12.**

GETTING THE POINT

Students will
◆ learn to listen for God's commands,
◆ plan ways to share God's message, and
◆ ask God to free them to live out their faith.

THIS LESSON AT A GLANCE

Before the lesson, collect the necessary items from the Learning Lab for the activities you plan to use. Refer to the pictures in the margin to see what each item looks like.

SECTION	MINUTES	WHAT STUDENTS WILL DO	LEARNING LAB SUPPLIES	CLASSROOM SUPPLIES
ATTENTION GRABBER	up to 10	**On Your Mark, Get Set...?**—Watch for a specific signal to start a race.	Two-toned superball, neon shoelaces	
BIBLE EXPLORATION AND APPLICATION	up to 15	**Wilderness Quiet**—Isolate themselves and consider Luke 3:2b-4.	Cassette: "Wilderness Quiet"	Bible, cassette player
	up to 13	**Ready and Waiting**—Work in groups to re-create John the Baptist's message from Luke 3:3-6.	Cassette: "Silent Night"	Bibles, "Get Ready, Get Ready!" handouts (p. 32), scissors, newsprint, markers, cassette player
	up to 12	**Attention, Please!**—Explore various Scriptures, and plan ways to draw people's attention to God.	Noisemaker, whip whistle, handblasters, clacker balls, bottle rings	Bibles
CLOSING	up to 10	**Untied**—Wrap the wrists of "prisoners," and name things that keep them from living out their faith.	Neon shoelaces	

Remember to make photocopies of the "Table Talk" handout (p. 33) to send home with your kids. "Table Talk" is a valuable tool for helping fifth- and sixth-graders talk with their parents about what they're learning in class.

THE LESSON

As kids arrive, teach them the signal for the quarter. Tell kids that whenever you sound the *noisemaker,* they're to stop what they're doing and look at you without talking. Explain that when you have everyone's attention, you'll continue the lesson.

Before you begin the lesson, ask kids about last week's "Table Talk" discussions. Use questions such as "How were you able to overcome specific sin in your life?" and "What did you learn about your family's reasons for obeying God?" However, be careful not to alienate students whose families chose not to use the "Table Talk."

ATTENTION GRABBER

LEARNING LAB

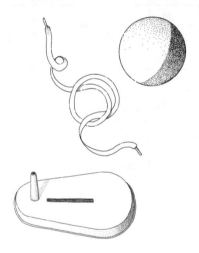

ON YOUR MARK, GET SET ...?

(up to 10 minutes)

Have kids form two teams. Have the teams line up along opposite walls of the room. Divide the room in half by laying the four *neon shoelaces* from the Learning Lab end to end across the middle of the floor.

Say: **When I give the signal, each of you should run to the center of the room, touch a shoelace with one foot, and then run back to your own wall. I'll start you by holding one arm straight out and dropping this *two-toned superball.* I'll say, "On your mark, get set..." and then I'll drop the ball. Don't go until I drop the superball and it touches the floor. OK? Here we go!**

Have kids crouch down as you say: **On your mark, get set...** Then toss the *two-toned superball* in the air about six inches, but catch it before it falls.

Several kids will probably fall forward in a false start. Call a false start, and have kids go back to the wall. Repeat the starting sequence, but this time drop the ball and quickly catch it with your other hand before it hits the floor. Call a false start again. This time hold the ball and pretend to deliberately toss it at the floor—but don't let go of it. Finally, drop the ball, and let the kids complete the race. Then ask:

- **Why did we have all those false starts?**
- **Why were you all paying such close attention to me just now?**
- **What other times do you pay really close attention**

as you wait for a signal or a message?

◆ **Have you ever waited for a signal or message from God? Explain.**

Say: **God is wonderful and powerful and can do great things in our lives. But first he has to have our attention—the way I had your attention just a moment ago. Today we're going to find out how** **we can prepare for Jesus' coming by living out our faith. The first step in living out our faith is giving God our attention.**

Return the *two-toned superball* and *neon shoelaces* to the Learning Lab.

BIBLE EXPLORATION AND APPLICATION

WILDERNESS QUIET

(up to 15 minutes)

Say: **We're going to begin our Bible study today with a pretend field trip. Scatter around the room so you're not close to anyone. Sit down in a comfortable position and be perfectly quiet. Pretend that we're suddenly transported back in time to the wilderness where John the Baptist preached. I'll play a tape that describes what you'd hear if you were there. Pretend you're alone in that wilderness with John the Baptist. When the tape ends, I'll read today's Bible passage, then we'll have a few more moments of quiet for you to think about what I read. Don't talk or move until I say time's up.**

After kids are settled and quiet, play the "Wilderness Quiet" segment of the *cassette tape.* When it ends, read **Luke 3:2b-4,** wait another ten seconds, and then say: **Time's up. Please form trios.**

Ask trios to discuss:

◆ **What was it like to be totally silent?**

◆ **How many waking minutes or hours a week would you say you're perfectly quiet and still?**

◆ **How many waking minutes or hours a week would you say you're totally alone?**

◆ **How do you think living alone in the wilderness affected John's relationship with God?**

◆ **How do you think your life would change if you spent ten minutes each day reading your Bible and being quiet and alone with God?**

LEARNING LAB

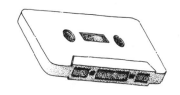

LEARNING LAB

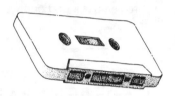

⎯ **BIBLE** *INSIGHT*

John didn't go to the wilderness to escape public attention. He went to *draw* attention to himself and his message. His ministry recalled that of the prophet Elijah, and he emphasized the parallels. Both men preached repentance. Both challenged a complacent religious community. Both came out of the wilderness (Judea and Gilead) and lived very simple and humble lifestyles. John's lifestyle helped build his audience.

Invite kids to share insights from their trios. Then say: **God used John the Baptist to change many people's lives and to prepare the way for the coming of Christ.** ☞ **We can prepare for Jesus' coming by living out our faith. One important thing we can do to live out our faith is to draw back from the busyness of our lives and take time to be quiet with God. Then we, like John, will be ready to hear God's commands. Now let's see how we can make John's message relevant to our lives today.**

READY AND WAITING

(up to 13 minutes)

Before class, photocopy and cut out the four projects on the "Get Ready, Get Ready!" handout (p. 32). You'll need one handout copy for every twelve to sixteen kids.

Open your Bible to **Luke 3:3-6,** and ask a volunteer to read the passage aloud. Say: **Now let's see how to put the ideas we just heard to use.**

Form groups of four. Read the four choices from the "Get Ready, Get Ready!" handout (p. 32), and allow groups each to choose one of the four projects. Give each group the corresponding card from the handout. If you have more than four groups, it's OK to give the same card to more than one group. If you have fewer than twelve kids, form smaller groups and combine roles or use only one or two of the cards. Set out newsprint and markers.

Say: **In your group, decide who will be the reader, the director, the cheerleader, and the editor. The role descriptions are given on the cards. You'll have about five minutes to complete the job described on your card. Begin.**

As kids work, play the instrumental version of "Silent Night" on the *cassette tape.*

After five minutes, tell kids it's time to put the finishing touches on their projects. After one more minute, call time and turn off the tape. Have groups take turns performing or presenting their projects. Give each group a hearty round of applause. Then ask:

◆ **What was it like preparing and presenting your projects?**

◆ **What did you learn about John's message?**

◆ **Do you think John's message is still important today? Why or why not?**

◆ **What are other ways you could tell people about Jesus?**

Say: **It's important to remember that** **we can prepare for Jesus' coming. Preparing for Jesus' coming involves talking to people about Jesus in ways they can understand. John the Baptist did it, and so can we.**

ATTENTION, PLEASE!

(up to 12 minutes)

Ask for five volunteers and give each person one of the following gizmos: *noisemaker, whip whistle, handblasters, clacker balls,* and *bottle rings.* Say: **Volunteers, use your gizmos to attract attention from the rest of the group. For example, you could try different ways to swing the** *clacker balls* **or juggle the** *bottle rings.*

Give kids about twenty to thirty seconds to attract attention. Collect the Learning Lab items from the kids, and ask:

◆ **Volunteers, what was it like trying to attract attention?**

◆ **What attracted the rest of you to the volunteers' actions?**

Say: **John the Baptist had a unique lifestyle that grabbed people's attention.** Have a volunteer read **Matthew 3:1-6** as others follow along. Ask:

◆ **How did the way the volunteers attracted attention compare to the way John attracted attention?**

◆ **What would people today say about a preacher who lived in the desert, wore clothes made from camel's hair, and lived on locusts and honey?**

Say: **I don't know if we would draw people to God if we lived on bugs and wore animal skins as John did. But there are things we can do that will call people's attention to God.**

Have kids form four groups. A group can be one person. Assign each group one of the following Bible passages: **John 13:34-35; 2 Corinthians 9:11-14; Philippians 2:12-16;** and **1 Peter 2:11-12.**

Say: **Read your passage, and decide how living according to that passage could call people's attention to God.**

Allow several minutes for groups to read and discuss their passages. Kids may come to conclusions such as these:

◆ **John 13:34-35**—We can draw attention to God by not putting each other down.

◆ **2 Corinthians 9:11-14**—We can draw attention to God by donating our time to help the homeless.

◆ **Philippians 2:12-16**—We can draw attention to God by not complaining or arguing and by being shining examples of

LEARNING LAB

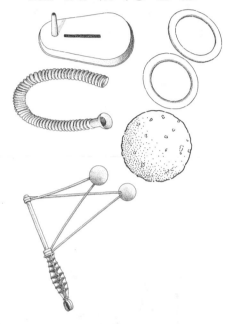

─KEY VERSE
CONNECTION

"For this reason Christ is the mediator of a new covenant, that those who are called may receive the promised eternal inheritance" (Hebrews 9:15a).

Kids tend to make and break promises on a regular basis. This Key Verse can help them understand the greatest promise of all—that faith in Jesus assures eternal blessings. Help kids hold on to that promise as they live out their faith in anticipation of Jesus' coming.

what Christians are like.

◆ **1 Peter 2:11-12**—We can draw attention to God by not cheating on tests.

Say:  **We can prepare for Jesus' coming, and these are some great ideas about how to live out our faith. Think about the lives of the people in this room. Without naming any names, tell what someone here has done to draw your attention to God.** Kids may give examples such as "She let me know she was praying for me when I had a problem," "He always cares about how other people feel," or "He always sees the best in people."

Say: **It's great to hear how you've encouraged each other! But there are probably very few of us who feel we can be the shining examples we'd like to be. And that brings us right back to the core of John's message: With God's help, we can change our hearts and lives to get ready for Jesus and to help others get ready for Jesus.**

TABLE TALK

Christian education extends beyond the classroom into the home. Photocopy the "Table Talk" handout (p. 33) for this week, and send it home with your kids. Encourage kids and parents to use the handout to spark meaningful discussion on this week's topic. Follow up next week by asking kids how their discussions with their families went.

CLOSING

LEARNING LAB

UNTIED

(up to 10 minutes)

Have kids form four groups, and ask each group to choose a "prisoner." Give each group a *neon shoelace.*

Say: **Have your prisoner hold out his or her hands with the wrists crossed. Take turns naming things that keep us busy and prevent us from living out our faith, such as too much homework or spending too much time watching television. For each thing you name, loosely**

wrap the shoelace once around the prisoner's wrists.

When all the prisoners' wrists are wrapped up, say: **Now, in each group, everyone reach out and hold your prisoner's hands. Let's pray. Dear Lord, we know it's easy to get tied up with all kinds of things that trap us. We want to  prepare for Jesus' coming. Help us escape from the trap of busyness and take time to hear your commands. In Jesus' name, amen.**

Have each group free its prisoner and throw its shoelace in the air to celebrate the freedom Jesus gives us to live out our faith.

Collect the *neon shoelaces* for use in later lessons.

 THE **POINT**

TEACHER TIP

Make sure kids don't wrap the shoelaces so tightly they cut off the circulation of the prisoners.

GET READY, GET READY!

Get-Ready Pantomime

Reader: Read aloud John's message in Luke 3:3-6.

Director: Help your group create and perform a pantomime, illustrating John's message. Tell kids why it's important to prepare for Jesus to come into their lives.

Cheerleader: As the passage is read aloud, make sure everyone has a part in the mime show.

Editor: Take notes on the newsprint, and write everyone's actions as you plan the show.

Get-Ready Newspaper Ad

Reader: Read aloud John's message in Luke 3:3-6.

Director: Help your group design and write a full-page newspaper ad or a giant Christmas card based on John's message, telling kids why it's important to prepare for Jesus to come into their lives.

Cheerleader: Make sure everyone contributes ideas.

Editor: Take notes on the newsprint, and write the ad or card in its final form.

Get-Ready Commercial

Reader: Read aloud John's message in Luke 3:3-6.

Director: Help your group write and perform a TV commercial based on John's message, telling kids why it's important to prepare for Jesus to come into their lives.

Cheerleader: Make sure everyone contributes ideas.

Editor: Take notes on the newsprint, and write the commercial in its final form.

Get-Ready Song Lyrics

Reader: Read aloud John's message in Luke 3:3-6.

Director: Help your group write song lyrics based on John's message, using a familiar song. Tell kids why it's important to prepare for Jesus to come into their lives.

Cheerleader: Make sure everyone contributes ideas.

Editor: Take notes on the newsprint, and write the lyrics for the song in its final form.

Discussion Starters

- What can you do to prepare for the day you meet Jesus face to face?
- What do you think Jesus expects from you while you are on earth?
- Do you think preparing to meet Jesus is more important than a combat mission? Why or why not?

Family Building

*For Kids Only: Think about what you'll want to tell or ask Jesus when you see him face to face. Write your message in a letter to God. When you finish, pray your letter aloud to God.

*For Parents Only: Take opportunities to help your children understand that preparing for meeting Jesus is much more than being good. Help them see that the "training" they're participating in also involves developing a relationship with Jesus and showing his love to others.

*For the Family: Talk about what it means to have faith in Christ. Let every person in your family have an opportunity to explain if he or she will go to heaven and why he or she thinks so. Use the following verses to help you in your discussion: John 3:16; Romans 3:22-24; 6:22-23; and Ephesians 2:8-10.

Something to Think About

The elite Army Rangers go through incredible training to prepare for some of the most dangerous combat missions in the world. Trainees begin every day with a five-mile run. They move on to the confidence course where they climb a thirteen-foot log fence (without ropes), crawl through eighty-two feet of mud covered by barbed wire, cross another mud pit on rafters thirty-two feet above the pit, crawl up a high rope net, and slide down a rope. This course serves as a warm-up for the next three to four hours where trainees practice hand-to-hand combat. Trainees are allowed to have only about three hours of sleep and one meal a day. But instead of ending with a cool shower and a long nap, trainees go to the classrooms to learn patrolling and leadership skills. They then take a "short nap" and do it all over again.

We have a mission that is much more important than any Army Ranger mission. One day we'll see Jesus face to face, and our mission is to get ready for that very important meeting.

"For physical training is of some value, but godliness has value for all things, holding promise for both the present life and the life to come"

(1 Timothy 4:8).

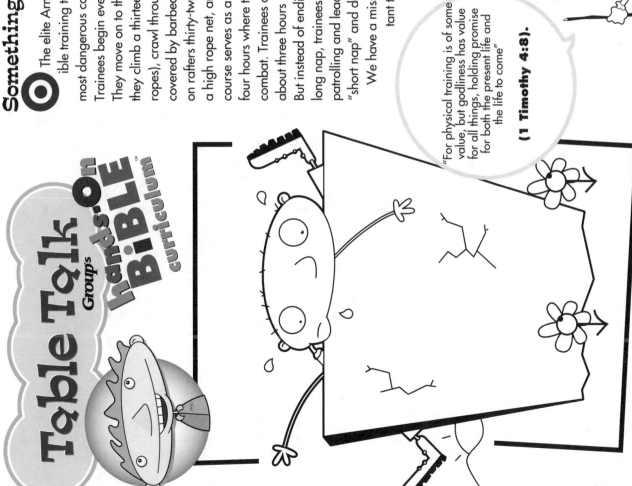

Table Talk

Group's hands-On BiBLE Curriculum™

John's Message, Week 2

CELEBRATING JESUS' BIRTH

THE POINT

☞ **Jesus' birth is something to celebrate!**

THE BIBLE BASIS

Luke 2:1-20

In those days Caesar Augustus issued a decree that a census should be taken of the entire Roman world. (This was the first census that took place while Quirinius was governor of Syria.) And everyone went to his own town to register.

So Joseph also went up from the town of Nazareth in Galilee to Judea, to Bethlehem the town of David, because he belonged to the house and line of David. He went there to register with Mary, who was pledged to be married to him and was expecting a child. While they were there, the time came for the baby to be born, and she gave birth to her firstborn, a son. She wrapped him in cloths and placed him in a manger, because there was no room for them in the inn.

And there were shepherds living out in the fields nearby, keeping watch over their flocks at night. An angel of the Lord appeared to them, and the glory of the Lord shone around them, and they were terrified. But the angel said to them, "Do not be afraid. I bring you good news of great joy that will be for all the people. Today in the town of David a Savior has been born to you; he is Christ the Lord. This will be a sign to you: You will find a baby wrapped in cloths and lying in a manger."

Suddenly a great company of the heavenly host appeared with the angel, praising God and saying, "Glory to God in the highest, and on earth peace to men on whom his favor rests."

When the angels had left them and gone into heaven, the shepherds said to one another, "Let's go to Bethlehem and see this thing that has happened, which the Lord has told us about."

So they hurried off and found Mary and Joseph, and the baby, who was lying in the manger. When they had seen him, they spread the word concerning what had been told them about this child, and all who heard it were amazed at what the shepherds said to them. But Mary treasured up all these things and pondered them in her heart. The shepherds returned, glorifying and praising God for all the things they had heard and seen, which were just as they had been told.

KEY *VERSE*
for Lessons 1–4

"For this reason Christ is the mediator of a new covenant, that those who are called may receive the promised eternal inheritance."

(Hebrews 9:15a)

The story is simple, yet incredibly profound. A young woman gives birth; God takes on the form of a human baby. The God whose awesome judgment rained fire and destruction on his enemies lay small and vulnerable in a feeding trough. God with us! For Mary, Joseph, and the shepherds, it must have seemed that the universe had turned upside down.

Fifth- and sixth-graders know the agony of being vulnerable; their universe turns upside down on a regular basis. To be made an outsider by an "in" group, to blush in mortal embarrassment over a slip of the tongue, to wear the wrong thing at the wrong time, to fail miserably in sports when the world is watching and all your friends are counting on you—these are just some of the emotional traumas ten- to twelve-year-olds face.

Use this lesson to show them that they don't have to face trouble alone: God is with us! That's really something to celebrate!

Other Scriptures used in this lesson are **Matthew 4:12-17; Colossians 4:3-6;** and **Isaiah 9:1-3, 6.**

GETTING THE POINT

Students will
◆ experience the period of waiting between the prophecy and fulfillment of Christ's birth,
◆ understand that Jesus' birth is a time of celebration,
◆ learn that celebration should last longer than the holiday, and
◆ discuss and understand how Jesus' birth changed the world.

THIS LESSON AT A GLANCE

Before the lesson, collect the necessary items from the Learning Lab for the activities you plan to use. Refer to the pictures in the margin to see what each item looks like.

SECTION	MINUTES	WHAT STUDENTS WILL DO	LEARNING LAB SUPPLIES	CLASSROOM SUPPLIES
ATTENTION GRABBER	up to 12	**400 Years in the Dungeon**—Listen to a taped story, then explore Matthew 4:12-17.	Fiber optic flashlight, cassette: "400 Years in the Dungeon"	Bible, cassette player
BIBLE EXPLORATION AND APPLICATION	up to 13	**Birth Announcement**—Create birth announcements for Jesus based on the elements found in Luke 2:1-20.		Bibles, paper, markers
	up to 12	**Year-Round Celebration**—Read Luke 2:20, and discuss ways to celebrate Jesus' birth throughout the year.	Handblasters	Bibles
	up to 13	**What Was It Like?**—Using simulation situations and various Scriptures, compare life before and after Christ's birth.	Package of spices, fiber optic flashlight, noisemaker	Bibles, "Another Life" handouts (p. 42), scissors, small plastic bag, paper, pencils
CLOSING	up to 10	**A Joy to Share**—Listen to a Christmas song, and pray for someone who needs to hear the message of it.	Cassette: "Joy to the World," "Lyrics Poster"	Cassette player

Remember to make photocopies of the "Table Talk" handout (p. 43) to send home with your kids. "Table Talk" is a valuable tool for helping fifth- and sixth-graders talk with their parents about what they're learning in class.

THE LESSON

As kids arrive, teach them the signal for the quarter. Tell kids that whenever you sound the *noisemaker*, they're to stop what they're doing and look at you without talking. Explain that when you have everyone's attention, you'll continue the lesson.

Before you begin the lesson, ask kids about last week's "Table Talk" discussions. Use questions such as "What did you learn about your relationship with Jesus?" and "How did your letter to God help your faith?" However, be careful not to alienate students whose families chose not to use "Table Talk."

ATTENTION GRABBER

400 YEARS IN THE DUNGEON

(up to 12 minutes)

Ask your kids to sit in a circle. Darken the room as much as possible, and instruct your kids to close their eyes as they listen to a segment of the *cassette tape*. It is vital they keep their eyes closed. Stress this! Tell kids they are not to open their eyes until you tap them individually on the shoulder.

Play "400 Years in the Dungeon" from the *cassette tape*.

After the tape draws to a close, stand behind the circle and walk around it, positioning the *fiber optic flashlight* in front of students' faces and tapping them on a shoulder one at a time. As kids open their eyes, indicate they should stay silent. Move around the circle until every student's eyes are open. Ask:

◆ **How does it feel to wait in line at the drive-through when you're hungry?**

◆ **How long can you wait for something you really want or need?**

◆ **What are some things you hate to wait for?**

Read **Matthew 4:12-17** aloud. Say: **God's people waited four hundred years from the time the last prophet spoke to the time Jesus arrived.**

Ask students to form pairs and discuss:

◆ **What's a time you've felt like you were waiting in the darkness for something? What were you waiting for?**

◆ **How was the story on the tape like God's people waiting in the dark for Jesus to appear?**

◆ **How did it feel to have the light flashed in your face after being in darkness?**

◆ **How is that light like Jesus' appearance after a wait of four hundred years?**

◆ **How would you feel if you waited for four hundred years for something, and then it happened?**

◆ **How did God's people feel when Jesus appeared?**

Say: **Not everyone recognized that Jesus was the long-awaited Messiah. But those who did knew that ☞ Jesus' birth is something to celebrate!**

Return the *cassette tape* and *fiber optic flashlight* to the Learning Lab for later use.

LEARNING LAB

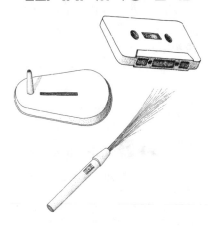

 ☞ THE **POINT**

——BIBLE *INSIGHT*

The book of Luke makes it clear that the reason Mary and Joseph traveled the eighty miles from Nazareth to their ancestral home of Bethlehem was to comply with the census of Caesar Augustus. There is evidence in Egyptian records that this census was actually the Roman census of 8 to 7 B.C., which was delayed in the Jewish province.

THE **POINT**

LEARNING LAB

BIBLE EXPLORATION AND APPLICATION

BIRTH ANNOUNCEMENT

(up to 13 minutes)

Have kids form groups of three, and distribute paper and markers to the groups. Divide the reading of **Luke 2:1-20** into three sections—verses 1-7, 8-14, 15-20—and assign one section to each group. Have groups each read their sections of the Luke passage aloud in their groups. Then have group members discuss what kind of birth announcement they could create that would let others know about the joy of Jesus' birth. Finally, have the group create an announcement using markers and paper.

After groups have finished their announcements, have a representative from each group present his or her group's birth announcement to the whole class. After groups have presented, ask:

◆ **What was it like to create a birth announcement for Jesus?**

◆ **What part of your group's announcement is most meaningful to you? Why?**

◆ **How could your birth announcement help you share Jesus' birth with someone who doesn't know Jesus?**

Say: **When you were born, your parents probably made some kind of birth announcement to family and friends. And you probably don't think much about that announcement now. But**  **Jesus' birth is something to celebrate, and there's no reason we can't celebrate his birth all year long!**

YEAR-ROUND CELEBRATION

(up to 12 minutes)

Have a volunteer read **Luke 2:20** as others follow along.

Say: **After the shepherds saw Jesus, they returned home and praised God.** Ask:

◆ **How do you think God's people may have celebrated when they heard the news of Jesus' birth?**

Show your kids the *handblasters* and say: **The shepherds praised God. We're going to use these *handblasters* as a** way to praise God for Jesus' birth. I'm going to pass the *handblasters* to someone in the circle. That person will say one way we can celebrate Jesus' birth during the year, such as giving money to poor people. Then the first person will smack the *handblasters* together and pass them to someone else. We'll continue until each person has had an opportunity to say how we can celebrate Jesus' birth during the year.

Pass the *handblasters* to a student. Continue until all the kids have had a chance to say one way to celebrate Jesus' birth throughout the year. Ask:

◆ **How did using the *handblasters* make you think about celebrating?**

◆ **Why do people think Jesus' birth is worth celebrating?**

◆ **What would your friends think if you celebrated Jesus' birth all year long?**

◆ **How will you celebrate one of these ideas?**

Say: ☞ **Jesus' birth is something to celebrate. When Jesus came to earth, it was a one-of-a-kind event. There's never been anything like it before or since, and that's reason to celebrate all year. But what would life have been like for the people who experienced Jesus' birth? Let's find out.**

Collect the *handblasters* to use in later lessons.

WHAT WAS IT LIKE?

(up to 13 minutes)

Before class photocopy the "Another Life" handout (p. 42), and cut apart the situations. Put the *package of spices* in a small plastic bag.

Form three groups. Have each group pick a reader to read the Bible passage, a scribe to write down the group's answers, an encourager to urge group members to participate, and a reporter to report the group's findings to the rest of the class. Have extra students serve as encouragers. If you have fewer than twelve kids, have the groups assign more than one role to a person. For example, the scribe could also be the reporter.

Distribute the situations from the "Another Life" handout, and give each group a pencil and a sheet of paper. Give the group with Situation 1 the *package of spices,* the group with Situation 2 the *fiber optic flashlight,* and the group with Situation 3 a *noisemaker.*

Tell kids they'll have five minutes to read their group's situation and discuss the questions. Tell them to be prepared to

---

TEACHER TIP

You may need to demonstrate the use of the *handblasters.* Hold one in your palm and bounce the other off the one in your palm. They make a loud pop, just like a cap gun. The harder the *handblasters* strike together, the louder they pop; but don't worry—they don't hurt you.

☞ THE **POINT**

LEARNING LAB

tell the rest of the class about their discoveries. While the groups are working, circulate around the room to assist any groups having difficulties.

After five minutes, have groups report their discoveries.

After groups have shared, ask:

◆ **How do you think the people who were there when Jesus was born felt when they learned he was the Messiah? Explain.**

◆ **How do you think their lives were changed?**

Say: **Many people praised God and celebrated when Jesus was born.** 🎵 **Jesus' birth is something to celebrate! So let's celebrate now by singing a Christmas song for Jesus.**

Collect the *package of spices, fiber optic flashlight,* and *noisemaker* for use in later lessons.

TABLE TALK

Christian education extends beyond the classroom into the home. Photocopy the "Table Talk" handout (p. 43) for this week, and send it home with your kids. Encourage kids and parents to use the handout to spark meaningful discussion on this week's topic. Follow up next week by asking kids how their discussions with their families went.

LEARNING LAB

CLOSING

A JOY TO SHARE

(up to 10 minutes)

Say: 🎵 **Jesus' birth is something to celebrate! You're probably used to celebrating Jesus' birth every Christmas. But there are others who may not know the true meaning of Christmas—God sending his Son.**

Have kids gather in a semicircle around the "Lyrics Poster." Say: **I'm going to play "Joy to the World," a song we sing every Christmas. Let's sing it together. The lyrics are here on our "Lyrics Poster."** Play "Joy to the World" from the *cassette tape.* When the song ends, have kids form pairs and discuss:

◆ **What words from "Joy to the World" would you like to share with someone who doesn't know the real meaning of Christmas?**

◆ **What ways could you share with this person?**

Say: **Sharing the real meaning of Christmas with someone who doesn't know it is one of the best Christmas gifts you could give. Take a few minutes and pray with your partner, asking God to help you share Jesus' birth with someone so they, too, can realize ☞ Jesus' birth is something to celebrate!**

Give kids a few minutes to pray before closing with "amen." Return the *cassette tape* and "Lyrics Poster" to the Learning Lab for future use.

ANOTHER LiFE

Photocopy and cut apart these situations. Give a situation and its corresponding Learning Lab item to each group.

SITUATION 1—Your group lives in a country with no spices or seasonings. You don't have salt or ketchup for your french fries or butter for your baked potatoes. People in your country eat their food plain.
- ◆ What would your lives be like without seasoning for your food?

One day someone brought spices to your country. This discovery transformed your country. Pass the *package of spices* around your group, and let each group member smell them. Then pass the spices around again, and let each group member take a small pinch to taste.
- ◆ How will living in your country be different now that you've discovered spices?

Read Colossians 4:3-6 and answer these questions:
- ◆ What does it mean to live "seasoned" lives?
- ◆ How is unseasoned food like the way people lived before Jesus came?
- ◆ How is seasoned food like the life we have since Jesus came?

SITUATION 2—Your group lives in a country where there are no light bulbs, and the buildings have no windows. When people go inside, they have to feel their way around because it's impossible to see.
- ◆ What would it be like to live in a country with no inside light?

One day, someone brought a *fiber optic flashlight* to your country. The people were impressed. They started planning ways they could do things inside their homes since now they had flashlights. Pass the *fiber optic flashlight* around and have each group member look at the different types of light coming from it.
- ◆ How will living in your country be different now that you've discovered the *fiber optic flashlight?*

Read Isaiah 9:1-3, 6 and answer these questions:
- ◆ What does it mean to live in darkness?
- ◆ How is walking in darkness like life before Jesus was born?
- ◆ How is having light from the *fiber optic flashlight* like life since Jesus was born?

SITUATION 3—Your group lives in a country with no sound. It's not that the people can't hear; it's just that no one has any need to make sound. All communication is done through touch and through sign language.
- ◆ What would it be like to live in a country with no sound?

One day, someone brought a *noisemaker* to your country. All the people were amazed. They had never heard anything before. Pass the *noisemaker* around and let each group member make noise with it.
- ◆ How will life change now that the people of your country have discovered sound?

Read Luke 2:13-15 and answer these questions:
- ◆ How did sound change the shepherds' lives?
- ◆ How is a world without sound like the world before Jesus was born?
- ◆ How is a world with sound like life since Jesus was born?

Table Talk

Group's hands-On BiBLE™ curriculum

"I bring you good news of great joy that will be for all the people. Today in the town of David a Savior has been born to you; he is Christ the Lord." **(Luke 2:10b-11).**

Celebrating Jesus' Birth, Week 3

Something to Think About

In the Philippine Islands, Christmas is celebrated for twenty-two days. The celebration begins with a church service at four in the morning on December 16 and continues until January 6. In India, servants present a lemon to the head of the household on Christmas morning to show their high esteem for the person. Rather than waiting for Santa Claus to come Christmas Eve, Syrian children set a bowl of water and wheat outside the house as they wait for one of the Magi's camels to bring them presents. Instead of decorating a Christmas tree, Italians decorate the Presepio which is made of strips of wood that form shelves. Presents, candy, and nuts are placed on the shelves. On St. Nicholas Eve in France, Pere Noel visits the homes of children and stuffs gifts in their shoes.

Jesus' birth is indeed something to celebrate. Christmas is a time to remember what God did for us by sending his Son to die for a lost and hurting world. So enjoy the traditions your family celebrates. But don't forget why you are celebrating. Whether you put the trimmings around the Presepio, leave your shoes out for Pere Noel, or wait excitedly for presents from the Magi's camel, remember the ultimate gift that was given for you—the life and death of God's Son, Jesus.

Discussion Starters

What do you think God likes about the Christmas celebrations in our country?

What do you think God dislikes about our Christmas celebrations?

What is the best way to celebrate Jesus' birth?

Family Building

*For Kids Only: Ask a friend at school what he or she does to celebrate Christmas. Then tell the person what your family does and why they do it.

*For Parents Only: Encourage your children to give a gift to someone who doesn't have money to buy Christmas gifts. Challenge your kids to save up enough money to buy the present or ask them to help you pick the present out.

*For the Family: Think of a new family tradition that directly reminds you of what Christmas is all about. For example, consider visiting a lonely neighbor for thirty minutes on Christmas Day, inviting friends over who have nowhere else to go, or reading Luke 2:1-20 aloud together.

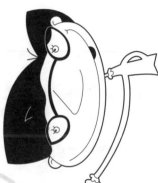

JESUS, OUR EXAMPLE

THE POINT

☞ **Becoming like Jesus means caring about others.**

THE BIBLE BASIS

Philippians 2:1-11

If you have any encouragement from being united with Christ, if any comfort from his love, if any fellowship with the Spirit, if any tenderness and compassion, then make my joy complete by being like-minded, having the same love, being one in spirit and purpose. Do nothing out of selfish ambition or vain conceit, but in humility consider others better than yourselves. Each of you should look not only to your own interests, but also to the interests of others.

Your attitude should be the same as that of Christ Jesus: Who, being in very nature God, did not consider equality with God something to be grasped, but made himself nothing, taking the very nature of a servant, being made in human likeness. And being found in appearance as a man, he humbled himself and became obedient to death—even death on a cross!

Therefore God exalted him to the highest place and gave him the name that is above every name, that at the name of Jesus every knee should bow, in heaven and on earth and under the earth, and every tongue confess that Jesus Christ is Lord, to the glory of God the Father.

If Paul were alive today, he could probably make a good living writing motivational books. Paul's words are convincing and compelling. He encourages an on-again, off-again audience to be diligent in becoming like Christ, to push beyond the comfort zone of day-to-day life.

Today's church is much the same as the church at Philippi. Our good will toward others seems to be expressed only when it's convenient for us. Yet, we preach a doctrine of constant service and love. Teach your fifth- and sixth-graders that caring for others involves more than the occasional service project. Help them cultivate ways to serve others daily in order to always "in humility consider others better than yourselves."

Another Scripture used in this lesson is **Philippians 2:13-18.**

KEY VERSE
for Lessons 1–4

"For this reason Christ is the mediator of a new covenant, that those who are called may receive the promised eternal inheritance."

(Hebrews 9:15a)

GETTING THE POINT

Students will
- understand the importance of caring for others,
- discover ways to care for those around them,
- identify the caring aspects of Jesus, and
- pray for opportunities to care.

THIS LESSON AT A GLANCE

Before the lesson, collect the necessary items from the Learning Lab for the activities you plan to use. Refer to the pictures in the margin to see what each item looks like.

SECTION	MINUTES	WHAT STUDENTS WILL DO	LEARNING LAB SUPPLIES	CLASSROOM SUPPLIES
ATTENTION GRABBER	up to 10	**Copy the Statue**—Explain how to copy a student's pose to someone who can't see the pose.		Sheet
BIBLE EXPLORATION AND APPLICATION	up to 15	**Peer Talk!**—Listen to how other kids feel about caring, and read Philippians 2:13-18.	Cassette: "Caring Collage"	Bibles, cassette player
	up to 12	**Creative Caring**—Show ways to care for others, and explore Philippians 2:1-8.	Noisemaker, package of spices, neon shoelaces, prism scope, fiber optic flashlight	Bibles, paper, pencils
	up to 15	**Caring Qualities**—Brainstorm ways Jesus cares, discover ways they can care for others, and examine Philippians 2:1-11.		Bibles, markers, newsprint
CLOSING	up to 8	**Caring Cords**—Commit to be caring in the same way God is caring.	Neon shoelaces	
MODULE REVIEW	up to 5	**Reflection**—Review what they've learned during the past four lessons.		Newsprint, marker

Remember to make photocopies of the "Table Talk" handout (p. 52) to send home with your kids. "Table Talk" is a valuable tool for helping fifth- and sixth-graders talk with their parents about what they're learning in class.

THE LESSON

As kids arrive, teach them the signal for the quarter. Tell kids that whenever you sound the *noisemaker,* they're to stop what they're doing and look at you without talking. Explain that when you have everyone's attention, you'll continue the lesson.

Before you begin the lesson, ask kids about last week's "Table Talk" discussions. Use questions such as "Were you able to get a gift for someone without one?" and "Were you able to start a new family tradition?" However, be careful not to alienate students whose families chose not to use "Table Talk."

ATTENTION GRABBER

LEARNING LAB

COPY THE STATUE

(up to 10 minutes)

Ask for two volunteers to be official "sheet-holders." Have them each grab one end of the sheet and hold it up like a flag. Depending on the size of the sheet, you may need to fold it over to make it easier to handle. Ask for two more volunteers, and have them stand on either side of the sheet. Have the sheet-holders lift the sheet to create a wall that separates the two volunteers.

The volunteers should be standing so neither of them can see the person on the other side of the sheet. Have the rest of the class sit on the floor where they can see both students standing by the sheet.

Have one of the volunteers act like a human statue and strike a pose, such as standing with arms flexed like a bodybuilder or standing on tiptoe with arms overhead like a ballet dancer.

Have the rest of the class members take turns explaining the pose to the other volunteer so that he or she can copy it exactly. Tell kids they can't demonstrate the pose; they can use words only to explain how to copy the human statue's position.

Give kids two minutes to explain how to copy the pose. Then drop the sheet so the two volunteers can see how closely they match. If you have time, repeat the poses with new volunteers.

Have the volunteers sit down with the rest of the class. Ask:

◆ **Was it hard or easy to get** (student's name) **to copy the pose exactly? Explain.**

◆ **What would have made it easier to explain how to**

TEACHER TIP

It's important to say The Point as it's written in each activity. Repeating The Point over and over throughout the lesson will help kids remember it and apply it to their lives.

TEACHER TIP

A dark sheet or blanket works best for this activity. Shade the room to prevent kids from being able to see each other through the sheet or blanket.

copy the human statue's pose?

◆ **How is the way our volunteer tried to copy the pose like the way people try to copy other people?**

◆ **What do people do to copy others?**

Say: **Lots of people work hard to become just like people they like or look up to. As Christians, we strive to become like Jesus. And today we're going to explore how** **becoming like Jesus means caring about others.**

☜ THE **POINT**

BIBLE EXPLORATION AND APPLICATION

PEER TALK!

(up to 15 minutes)

Tell kids to get in a comfortable position. Then play the "Caring Collage" section of the *cassette tape* from the Learning Lab. In this tape segment, fifth- and sixth-graders talk about what caring means to them, and they describe a time they felt cared for.

After the tape segment ends, have kids form pairs. Have them tell each other about a time from their own experiences when they felt cared for or when they cared for someone else. Then have partners read **Philippians 2:13-18** together, and answer the following questions:

◆ **What goes through your mind when you care for someone else?**

◆ **How would you feel if someone complained while they did something caring for you?**

◆ **How can caring for others make Christians "shine like stars"?**

◆ **Why does caring for others please God?**

Ask volunteers to tell the class what they discovered with their partners.

Say: **Becoming like Jesus means caring about others. Caring for others is an expression of love. And by doing loving things for others, we show the entire world what it means to be loved by God. Let's brainstorm creative ways to care.**

LEARNING LAB

KEY VERSE
CONNECTION

"For this reason Christ is the mediator of a new covenant, that those who are called may receive the promised eternal inheritance" (Hebrews 9:15a).

Fifth- and sixth-graders may find it awkward to express care and concern for others. The impulse may be there, but it's hard for kids to be demonstrative at that age. Let this Key Verse encourage kids to accept the blessings that God offers and to pass them on to others.

☜ THE **POINT**

LEARNING LAB

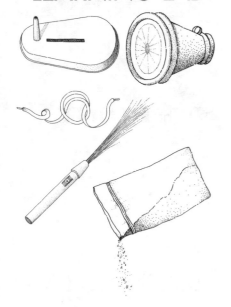

TEACHER TIP

Encourage active participation in the discussion by following up kids' answers with questions such as "What did you mean by that?" and "Can you tell me more?"

THE **POINT**

CREATIVE CARING

(up to 12 minutes)

Have kids sit in a circle on the floor. Put the *package of spices* in the middle of the circle. Have kids brainstorm ways the spices could be used to care for others. Then have each person demonstrate his or her caring action with another class member. For example, a student might pretend to cook a meal for a homeless person or use the spices as potpourri in a friend's closet.

Then place the *noisemaker, prism scope, neon shoelaces,* and *fiber optic flashlight* in the middle of your circle along with the spices. Have kids pass the other gizmos around the circle to one another and act out as many ideas as they can think of.

After several minutes, ask:

◆ **Was it hard to think of ways to care for others with the gizmos? Why or why not?**

◆ **Is it hard to think of ways to care for others in real life? Why or why not?**

Collect the Learning Lab items for use in later lessons.

Have kids form trios. Distribute a sheet of paper and a pencil to each trio. In their trios have kids choose a reader who will read the Bible verse aloud, a scribe who will take notes, and a reporter who will report the trio's discoveries to the rest of the class.

Say: **The Bible is a great place to look for caring ideas.** Ask the readers to read **Philippians 2:1-8** as the others follow along. Then have trios each come up with five ways they can care for others at home, at school, or at church. Kids might come up with ideas such as helping Mom with dinner, helping a friend with a tough homework assignment, or volunteering in the church nursery.

Give trios a couple of minutes for discussion, then have the reporters share their ideas with the rest of the class.

Say: **You have terrific ideas on how to care for one another. Jesus showed he cared for us when he came to earth and died for us. God's plan for us may not mean dying for others, but it does mean having the same attitude toward others that Jesus has. God wants us to become like Jesus, and**  **becoming like Jesus means caring about others. After we explore the caring qualities Paul talks about in Philippians, we'll think about ways we can show those characteristics.**

CARING QUALITIES

(up to 15 minutes)

Have kids form groups of three or four. Give each group markers and a sheet of newsprint. Tell each group to draw a vertical line to divide the sheet of newsprint in half. Then have groups think of caring things Jesus does for them. Have kids write the caring things or draw pictures of them on one side of the newsprint. Kids might write, "Answers my prayers," "Takes away my pain," or "Gives me peace."

Say: **Now let's look at the caring qualities Paul talks about in Philippians.** In each group have kids take turns reading aloud **Philippians 2:1-11,** verse by verse. Then have kids list on the other half of the newsprint all the caring qualities they find in the passage, such as tenderness and compassion.

Have groups share their lists with the whole class.

Point to the lists of caring qualities and ask:

◆ **Which of these things do you already do?**

◆ **Which of these things can you start doing?**

◆ **How can you do that?**

◆ **Is it possible for us to do all these things? Why or why not?**

◆ **How do we know when we're doing enough to care about others?**

Say: **When Jesus was on earth he cared about the people he was with. Now, even though he's in heaven, Jesus still cares about people. If we want to ☞ become like Jesus, we'll care about others, too.**

—**BIBLE** *INSIGHT*

Many scholars believe that **Philippians 2:5-11** is an early hymn or liturgical composition that Paul included in his letter. It is unknown whether Paul created the passage or whether God simply inspired him to use it in this letter.

☜ THE **POINT**

TABLE TALK

Christian education extends beyond the classroom into the home. Photocopy the "Table Talk" handout (p. 52) for this week, and send it home with your kids. Encourage kids and parents to use the handout to spark meaningful discussion on this week's topic. Follow up next week by asking kids how their discussions with their families went.

LEARNING LAB

THE **POINT**

CLOSING

CARING CORDS

(up to 8 minutes)

Have kids stand in a line. Tie the four *neon shoelaces* together. Hold one end of the shoelaces, and have kids each wrap it once around one of their wrists. If you have more than sixteen kids, it'll be easier to have kids hold the shoelaces instead of wrapping them around their wrists. Gently pull the shoelaces and lead kids around the room one time.

Then have kids form a circle, keeping their wrists wrapped in the shoelaces.

Say: **In the book of Hosea, God says he drew the people to him with "cords of human kindness" and with "ties of love." We can follow that example and bring the people we know to God by caring about them.**  **Becoming like Jesus means caring about others.**

Close in prayer, thanking God for his "ties of love" and asking him to give opportunities to care for others.

Collect the *neon shoelaces* for use in later lessons.

MODULE REVIEW

REFLECTION

(up to 5 minutes)

Say: **Today we've learned that**  **becoming like Jesus means caring about others. But during the past four class sessions, we've learned quite a bit about when Jesus came to earth and what that means for us today. Let's take a moment now to think about what we've gained from those class sessions.**

Form pairs. Write the following phrases on newsprint for kids to refer to, then have students take turns telling how they'd complete the sentences:

- ◆ "Obeying God faithfully means…"
- ◆ "One way I can prepare for Jesus' coming is…"
- ◆ "I can celebrate Jesus' birth by…"
- ◆ "One thing I can do to care for others is…"

When everyone responds, have pairs report how they completed the sentences.

To dismiss, have kids join together in an impromptu celebration of Jesus' birth with cheering, high fives, or a rousing a cappella version of "Joy to the World."

Discussion Starters

- Describe a time you did more than enough for a hurting friend or family member. How did it make you feel?
- Why do you think Florence Nightingale was so willing to go beyond the call of duty?
- How can you follow Florence's and Jesus' example of caring for others?

Family Building

*For Kids Only: Show your family how you care for them by committing to make dinner for the family once or twice a month. Ask your parents for any help you may need with getting started.

*For Parents Only: Help your children gain exposure to population groups that need special care. Take your family to volunteer at a nursing home, a homeless shelter, and another organization you choose. After volunteering once at each site, decide as a family which organization you'd like to volunteer regularly at.

*For the Family: Make a care package for a family member, a friend, or an acquaintance. Include things in the package that will demonstrate how you care for the person as an individual. For example, if the package is for a grandparent, include handmade cards and notes. If the package is for a neighbor, include a coupon that he or she can redeem to have you wash his or her car.

Something to Think About

Florence Nightingale couldn't believe what she was hearing from the medic: "The men are afraid to send their shirts to be washed, for fear they'll be stolen. I think only six shirts were washed and came back last month."

There were more than a thousand soldiers in the hospital. Florence knew the effects dirty linens and clothing could have on healing wounds. So she went to the town market and returned with cartloads of brand-new shirts.

"Where did these come from?" asked the supply officer.

"I bought them," said Florence. Florence didn't stop there. Using her own money, she rented a nearby house and hired soldiers' wives to wash the hospital bedding.

It would have been enough for Florence to simply do her job as a nurse. It would have been enough for her to put in an order for shirts and bedding with the supply officer. During her whole life, Florence did more than enough. She constantly gave her own money, time, and love to help others who were wounded, hurting, and dying.

"Suppose a brother or sister is without clothes and daily food. If one of you says to him, 'Go, I wish you well; keep warm and well fed,' but does nothing about his physical needs, what good is it?"

(James 2:15-16).

WHOOHOO!! CLEAN SHIRTS!!

Table Talk
Group's Hands-On Bible Curriculum™

Jesus, Our Example, Week 4

Permission to photocopy this handout from Group's Hands-On Bible Curriculum™ for Grades 5 and 6 granted for local church use. Copyright © Group Publishing, Inc., P.O. Box 481, Loveland, CO 80539.

RELATIONSHIPS

If you've spent any time with adolescents, you already know that relationships are incredibly important to kids in fifth and sixth grade.

When asked to rank the most important influences in their lives, Christian young people list parents; friends; church and ministers; grandparents, aunts, and uncles; youth leaders and Sunday school teachers; and school teachers. Television, records, movies, and magazines all fall below relationships.

Friends are powerful in influencing kids to do wrong—or right. So good relationships are vital to your kids' emotional and spiritual health.

This unit will help your kids sort through some of the troubling things in their relationships. Use these five lessons to help your kids develop relationship-building skills that will help them through the battles of early adolescence and prepare them for solid relationships in the years to come.

FIVE LESSONS ON RELATIONSHIPS

LESSON	PAGE	THE POINT	THE BIBLE BASIS
5—Handling Conflict	55	God shows us how to handle conflict.	Matthew 5:38-42
6—Forgiving Others	63	God wants us to forgive others as he's forgiven us.	Matthew 18:21-35
7—Between Guys and Girls	71	God helps guys and girls develop good friendships.	Ephesians 5:1-5
8—Standing Strong	80	God will honor us for standing strong.	Numbers 14:20-24
9—Building Others Up	89	God wants us to build people up.	1 Thessalonians 5:4-11

THE SIGNAL

During the lessons on relationships, your signal to get kids back together during activities will be sounding the *noise-maker* found in the Learning Lab. In response to sounding the *noisemaker,* have kids stop what they're doing and focus on you for their next instructions.

Tell kids about this signal before the lesson begins. Explain that it's important to respond to this signal quickly so the class can do as many fun activities as possible.

THE TIME STUFFER

The Time Stuffer for the five lessons on relationships is a poster called "Building Blocks for Blockbuster Relationships," which is found in the Learning Lab. Simply put it on the wall, and stock an area nearby with paper, pens or pencils, and markers. The directions on the poster instruct kids to do or create something that will help them strengthen a relationship.

Use the Time Stuffer to constructively occupy kids' time before your class starts, when some kids finish an activity earlier than others, or just when you have extra time with a few kids.

REMEMBERING THE BIBLE

Each four- or five-week module focuses on a Key Bible Verse. The Key Verse for this module is "So in everything, do to others what you would have them do to you" **(Matthew 7:12a).**

Look for the Key Verse Connection in the margin of each lesson to tie the Key Verse to that week's Point.

HANDLING CONFLICT

THE POINT

 God shows us how to handle conflict.

THE BIBLE BASIS

Matthew 5:38-42

> You have heard that it was said, "Eye for eye, and tooth for tooth." But I tell you, Do not resist an evil person. If someone strikes you on the right cheek, turn to him the other also. And if someone wants to sue you and take your tunic, let him have your cloak as well. If someone forces you to go one mile, go with him two miles. Give to the one who asks you, and do not turn away from the one who wants to borrow from you.

"Hurt him back!" is a common initial response when someone hurts us. Revenge is a natural human reaction, and sometimes it's hard to stop. But when we lash out with fists, words, or some other form of viciousness, we usually escalate the problem in the relationship instead of helping it.

Even small conflicts can grow into friendship-ending battles. And no one is affected by this sort of behavior more than young adolescents.

God has given us a different way to handle conflicts. By being less concerned about self and more concerned about the other person, we can use conflict to strengthen relationships instead of destroy them.

In this lesson, your kids will discover how to handle the conflicts that arise in their relationships.

Other Scriptures used in this lesson are **Matthew 5:43-48; Mark 15:1-5, 15-20; Luke 23:32-37; John 18:19-24;** and **2 Timothy 2:23-24.**

KEY VERSE
for Lessons 5–9

"So in everything, do to others what you would have them do to you."

(Matthew 7:12a)

GETTING THE POINT

Students will

◆ experience conflict and discuss how they feel about it,

◆ discover what Jesus said about how to handle conflicts,

◆ discuss examples of conflicts and how they were handled, and

◆ determine ways to respond constructively to conflict.

THIS LESSON AT A GLANCE

Before the lesson, collect the necessary items from the Learning Lab for the activities you plan to use. Refer to the pictures in the margin to see what each item looks like.

SECTION	MINUTES	WHAT STUDENTS WILL DO	LEARNING LAB SUPPLIES	CLASSROOM SUPPLIES
ATTENTION GRABBER	up to 10	**Impossible Game**—Play a game that's impossible to win.	Prism scopes, bottle rings	Masking tape
BIBLE EXPLORATION AND APPLICATION	up to 13	**Colossal Conflicts**—Discuss conflicts other kids have faced and then explore Matthew 5:38-42.	Cassette: "Conflicts"	Bibles, cassette player
	up to 12	**Ruckus War!**—Form teams and compete to see who can make the most noise and then explore 2 Timothy 2:23-24 with partners.	Handblasters, clacker balls, noisemakers, whip whistle	Bibles
	up to 15	**If Someone Hits You...**—Have someone sabotage their game, discuss their reactions, and examine Jesus' reactions during his last hours.	Bottle rings	Bibles, paper, pens or pencils
CLOSING	up to 10	**Let's Shake on It**—Try to shake people's hands while looking through a prism and then sing a song asking for God's help in resolving conflict.	Prism scopes, cassette: "Friends," "Lyrics Poster"	Cassette player

Remember to make photocopies of the "Table Talk" handout (p. 62) to send home with your kids. "Table Talk" is a valuable tool for helping fifth- and sixth-graders talk with their parents about what they're learning in class.

THE LESSON

As kids arrive, teach them the signal for the quarter. Tell kids that whenever you sound the *noisemaker,* they're to stop what they're doing and look at you without talking. Explain that when you have everyone's attention, you'll continue the lesson.

Before you begin the lesson, ask kids about last week's "Table Talk" discussions. Use questions such as "How were you able to help serve a meal for your family?" and "What was it like to volunteer to help others?" However, be careful not to alienate students whose families chose not to use "Table Talk."

ATTENTION GRABBER

IMPOSSIBLE GAME

2 posters — (Ring toss)

(up to 10 minutes)

Use masking tape to mark a line across the room, and have kids form two single file lines behind it. Place the two *prism scopes* on the floor at least five feet away from the line and about two feet apart.

Give the first person in each line two of the *bottle rings,* and give these instructions: **You've probably seen a ring-toss game like this at a carnival or an amusement park. The object is to toss the *bottle ring* so it loops around one of the *prism scopes.* Anyone who does it twice in a row is a winner.**

Let the first person try tossing two rings and then move on to the next person. Kids will enjoy the challenge at first but will soon start complaining that the game is impossible. Keep going until everyone has had two tosses.

Once you stop the game, collect the *prism scopes* and the *bottle rings* for use in later lessons. Then form pairs and have kids discuss the following questions. After each question is discussed, have volunteers share with the whole class what they talked about. Ask:

◆ **What's your reaction to this game? Explain.**

◆ **What feelings did you experience as you tossed the rings?**

◆ **How were your feelings similar to the way you sometimes feel about friendships that don't go the way you want them to?**

Say: **Today we're going to be talking about conflict.**

LEARNING LAB

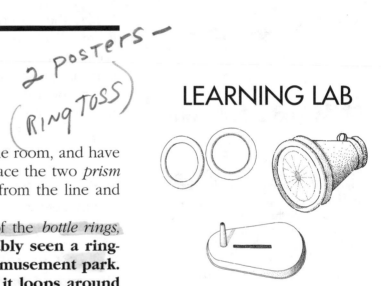

THE **POINT** ☞   **Conflict doesn't always have to end painfully.** ☞ **God shows us how to handle conflict, and we're going to see how today.**

BIBLE EXPLORATION AND APPLICATION

COLOSSAL CONFLICTS

(up to 13 minutes)

LEARNING LAB

Play the "Conflicts" segments from the *cassette tape,* one at a time. Each segment has one student telling about the worst conflict he or she has ever had, followed by a brief pause and that person's description of how the conflict worked out. You'll be directed to stop the tape before the conflict-resolution description for each segment. Have kids suggest ways of handling the conflict. Then play the tape and let kids hear how each conflict situation worked out.

Say: **We just heard how several kids worked out conflicts. Now let's see what Jesus says about conflict.** Have a volunteer read **Matthew 5:38-42** aloud as other students follow along. Form groups of no more than four, and tell kids to take turns answering the following questions. Ask:

◆ **Which of the kids resolved their conflicts in a way that would have pleased Jesus, according to this passage? Explain.**

◆ **How would showing the attitudes described in this Scripture passage help resolve conflicts?**

Say: ☞ **God shows us how to handle conflict by having the attitudes Jesus described in Matthew 5:38-42. The Bible also teaches about resolving conflicts in 2 Timothy 2:23-24. Let's explore the advice from 2 Timothy.**

━ **BIBLE** *INSIGHT*

The Gospel of Matthew is predominantly a Jewish gospel. Rather than explaining Jewish thoughts or phrases, Matthew assumes the reader is familiar with the Mosaic law. Therefore, Matthew doesn't expound with historical notes when Jesus refers to the law in his oft-repeated statement in the Sermon on the Mount: "You have heard that it was said…"

THE **POINT** ☞

LEARNING LAB

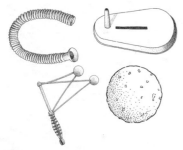

RUCKUS WAR!

(up to 12 minutes)

Form two teams. Place one team on your right and the other on your left. Give one team the *whip whistle,* a *noisemaker,* and a *handblaster.* Give the other team the *clacker balls,* a *noisemaker,* and a *handblaster.* Then say: **On "go," we're going to compete to see which team can make the** most noise. **You can use the Learning Lab items I gave you, but you can also use your hands, your feet, and your voices. The contest will consist of three rounds, each lasting ten seconds. During the rounds, you must make as much noise as possible to try to drown out the other team. At the end of each round, I will name the noisiest team. The team that wins two out of three rounds wins the competition.**

Proceed with the competition. After each round, name a winner. After three rounds, offer a round of applause to the winning team. Collect the Learning Lab items for later use. Then have kids form pairs, and discuss these questions:

◆ **What's your reaction to this competition?**

◆ **How did you feel trying to out-yell the other team?**

◆ **How is this competition similar to the way people sometimes handle conflict in real life?**

◆ **Do you ever respond to conflict by yelling at the other person? Why or why not?**

◆ **Instead of yelling, what's a better way to resolve conflicts with friends?**

Have partners read together **2 Timothy 2:23-24.** Ask partners to share conflicts they've handled well according to this passage. Tell partners to be sure to listen well and be ready to report to the class the good things their partners did to resolve the conflicts.

After a few minutes, have kids each tell the class the things their partners did in resolving the conflict. Give each person a round of applause for the good things he or she did.

When everyone has reported, say: **As we've seen from what you reported,** **God shows us how to handle conflict.**

[handwritten margin note:] Do any one who want to Share A conflict

---

▌ IF SOMEONE HITS YOU... 📖

(up to 15 minutes)

Form two teams. A team can be two people. Have teams move to opposite ends of the room and give each team two *bottle rings,* a pencil or pen, and a sheet of paper. Have teams assign half of their team members to be Tossers and the other half to be Catchers. In each team, have the Tossers and the Catchers line up facing each other about ten feet apart. The object is to have a Tosser toss a ring and a Catcher catch it. After one Tosser tosses the two rings, switch to a different Catcher and Tosser.

Say: **You'll have three minutes to toss the rings. The**

TEACHER TIP

Because this activity will reach a high noise level, it would be best to move this activity outside or to another area to avoid disturbing other classes nearby. If this will not work, limit the noise-making time to five seconds for each round.

TEACHER TIP

It's important to say The Point just as it's written in each activity. Repeating The Point over and over will help kids remember it and apply it to their lives.

 THE **POINT**

LEARNING LAB

KEY VERSE CONNECTION

"So in everything, do to others what you would have them do to you" (Matthew 7:12a).

Preadolescence is a time of roller coaster emotions. Kids are struggling to establish their own identities, both at home and at school. As a result, conflict may seem a daily part of life. Use this Key Verse to encourage kids to think about how they like to be treated and to treat others in the same way when conflicts arise.

THE POINT ☞

team with the most catches wins. Keep your own score on the sheet of paper I gave you.

When the teams get going, go to one team and ask if you can take a turn with one of the two rings. Toss it so that it's nearly impossible for the Catcher to catch. Then go to the other team and do the same. Take at least two turns with each team. If anyone offers you a second ring to toss, throw it much better. After the three minutes are up, call time and gather the *bottle rings* for later use.

When kids come back together, ask:

◆ **How did you like this game?**

◆ **How did you feel when I asked for a turn?**

◆ **What did you think when I messed up?**

◆ **How are the feelings you had like the feelings you sometimes get when friends do things you don't like?**

After the discussion, say: **It's easy to react with anger or frustration toward others. Let's take a look at what Jesus says about how we should handle real-life situations like these.**

Read aloud **Matthew 5:38-48.** Then ask:

◆ **According to this passage, what should we do in situations where others don't treat us the way we'd like?**

Say: **Jesus taught you should "turn the other cheek" when someone strikes you. Let's see how Jesus lived what he taught.**

Have kids form trios, and have each person read one of the following passages aloud: **John 18:19-24; Mark 15:1-5, 15-20;** and **Luke 23:32-37.** Have trios discuss the following questions:

◆ **How did Jesus react when he was flogged, beaten, mocked, and then nailed to a cross?**

◆ **What reactions should we have toward our enemies?**

◆ **How do you usually react when someone hurts you?**

◆ **How could Jesus' actions help you in the next conflict you face?**

When trios finish, ask a few volunteers to share what they discussed in their trios. Then say: **It's not always easy, but ☞ God shows us how to handle conflict. One way is by treating others with kindness and respect, even when they hurt you.**

TABLE TALK

Christian education extends beyond the classroom into the home. Photocopy the "Table Talk" handout (p. 62) for this week, and send it home with your kids. Encourage kids and parents to use the handout to spark meaningful discussion on this week's topic. Follow up next week by asking kids how their discussions with their families went.

CLOSING

LET'S SHAKE ON IT

(up to 10 minutes)

Have kids scatter throughout the room and then give two people each one of the *prism scopes*. On "go," have the kids with the *prism scopes* each hold the scope up to one eye, close the other eye, and then race through the room to see how many people's hands they can shake in ten seconds. When time is up, have them pass along the *prism scopes* to two new people and repeat the activity. Continue repeating the activity until everyone has given it a try. When everyone is finished, collect the *prism scopes* for later use, and have kids discuss these questions:

◆ **How is looking through the *prism scopes* while trying to shake hands like what happens when you don't resolve conflicts with friends?**

◆ **How can you make sure you resolve conflicts quickly with all your friends?**

Say: **Resolving conflict isn't easy. Our natural tendency is often to get back at the other person. But because 📖 God shows us how to handle conflict, we can enjoy the benefits of making our friendships strong and lasting.**

To close our class today, we're going to sing "Friends" to celebrate the friendships God has given us and to thank him for showing us how to handle conflict.

Display the "Lyrics Poster" from the Learning Lab and play the song "Friends" from the *cassette tape* for kids to sing along with.

End your time together with a prayer, asking God to help each person in your class handle conflicts constructively.

LEARNING LAB

How is this like Being mad at a Friend and not making mends

what have we learned Today that can Help us relsolve our promblems

🐟 THE **POINT** *Quickly*

Table Talk

Group's **hands-On BiBLE curriculum™**

Discussion Starters

- How do you deal with conflict with your family members? friends?
- What things do you need to do differently when it comes to conflict?
- What things would you like your family members to do differently?

Family Building

*For Kids Only: The next time you get angry with your parents, stop whatever you're doing and try to put yourself in their shoes. Really think about why your parents are responding that way.

*For Parents Only: Carefully examine the ways you model handling conflict to your kids. Ask them for forgiveness for your failures and explain to them how you should've responded.

*For the Family: Give every person in your family an opportunity to complete the following sentence: "It really bothers me when..." Carefully listen to each person's statement, and brainstorm ways to deal with the problem.

Something to Think About

Take this quiz to see how your family deals with conflict. Choose the answer that most closely matches your family:

1. When my parents ask me to clean my room, I:
   a. say "Of course, my darling parents. I live to please you."
   b. flick the dog's nose for making such a mess of my room.
   c. scream "I hate you! How can you be so cruel?" and then burst into tears.

2. When my child comes home with an F on an assignment, I:
   a. hug my child and say "Grades, shmades."
   b. call the principal and demand that the poor excuse for a teacher be fired.
   c. collect all my child's video games and have a big bonfire.

3. When I'm on a long drive and my little sister falls asleep, I:
   a. offer her my shoulder and gently kiss her head.
   b. shove her back up and laugh while her head bobs up and down.
   c. take her doll hostage while she sleeps and then demand a ransom.

Since you and every member in your family are human, conflict is inevitable. The key to a happy home is learning how to handle that conflict. There are three basic ways to deal with conflict: running away, falling apart, or coming together.

When you come together, you take time to listen to how the other people in your family feel and they take time to listen to you. You aren't worried about winning or being right. You're worried about understanding and being understood. You may not get your way after coming together on a conflict, but you will have a better understanding of why others feel the way they do. Conflict is often full of charged emotion, but coming together will help your family avoid crazy responses like the ones in the quiz.

"A hot-tempered man stirs up dissension, but a patient man calms a quarrel" **(Proverbs 15:18).**

OF COURSE, darling parents, I LIVE TO PLEASE YOU.

What a GREAT son we have dear!

YES, sweetie, he IS the GREATEST!

FORGIVING OTHERS

THE POINT

☞ **God wants us to forgive others as he's forgiven us.**

THE BIBLE BASIS

Matthew 18:21-35

Then Peter came to Jesus and asked, "Lord, how many times shall I forgive my brother when he sins against me? Up to seven times?"

Jesus answered, "I tell you, not seven times, but seventy-seven times.

"Therefore, the kingdom of heaven is like a king who wanted to settle accounts with his servants. As he began the settlement, a man who owed him ten thousand talents was brought to him. Since he was not able to pay, the master ordered that he and his wife and his children and all that he had be sold to repay the debt.

"The servant fell on his knees before him. 'Be patient with me,' he begged, 'and I will pay back everything.' The servant's master took pity on him, canceled the debt and let him go.

"But when that servant went out, he found one of his fellow servants who owed him a hundred denarii. He grabbed him and began to choke him. 'Pay back what you owe me!' he demanded.

"His fellow servant fell to his knees and begged him, 'Be patient with me, and I will pay you back.'

"But he refused. Instead, he went off and had the man thrown into prison until he could pay the debt. When the other servants saw what had happened, they were greatly distressed and went and told their master everything that had happened.

"Then the master called the servant in. 'You wicked servant,' he said, 'I canceled all that debt of yours because you begged me to. Shouldn't you have had mercy on your fellow servant just as I had on you?' In anger his master turned him over to the jailers to be tortured, until he should pay back all he owed.

"This is how my heavenly Father will treat each of you unless you forgive your brother from your heart."

Sometimes it's tough to forgive. There are people who just don't seem to deserve our forgiveness. Most fifth- and sixth-graders have a very strong sense of fairness. They're happy to

---
KEY VERSE
for Lessons 5–9

"So in everything, do to others what you would have them do to you."

(Matthew 7:12a)

see people "get what they deserve." They don't see the point of forgiving people who will just turn around and do the same thing again.

God's justice is different from ours. No one can measure up to God's standards, yet he willingly offers grace and forgiveness to anyone who asks. Since we're forgiven, we also need to forgive—over and over again. When we remember that the cost of our forgiveness was Jesus' death, it's easier to forgive the relatively small wrongs that are done to us. And when serious wrongs are committed against us, Jesus' example becomes that much more important.

Use this lesson to help your kids see that God wants them to forgive—even when it's hard.

Another Scripture used in this lesson is **Matthew 6:12-15.**

GETTING THE POINT

Students will
- ◆ think about the value of forgiving others,
- ◆ experience forgiveness using disappearing ink,
- ◆ create a skit demonstrating the lesson's Bible passage, and
- ◆ write stories about forgiveness.

THIS LESSON AT A GLANCE

Before the lesson, collect the necessary items from the Learning Lab for the activities you plan to use. Refer to the pictures in the margin to see what each item looks like.

SECTION	MINUTES	WHAT STUDENTS WILL DO	LEARNING LAB SUPPLIES	CLASSROOM SUPPLIES
ATTENTION GRABBER	up to 10	**All Tied Up**—Compare a knotted shoelace to unforgiveness in people's lives.	Neon shoelaces	
BIBLE EXPLORATION AND APPLICATION	up to 12	**Disappearing Unforgiveness**—Explore forgiveness using disappearing ink and read Matthew 6:12-15.	Disappearing ink	Bibles, paper
	up to 15	**Like God Forgives**—Read Matthew 18:21-35 and create skits that put Scripture into a modern setting.		Bibles
	up to 13	**Obey the Parable**—Write true-to-life stories based on the forgiveness described in Matthew 18:21-22.		Bibles, paper, pens or pencils
CLOSING	up to 10	**Aroma of Forgiveness**—Try to smell spices with their noses plugged and then talk about the importance of forgiving others.	Package of spices	

Remember to make photocopies of the "Table Talk" handout (p. 70) to send home with your kids. "Table Talk" is a valuable tool for helping fifth- and sixth-graders talk with their parents about what they're learning in class.

THE LESSON

When kids arrive, remind them that you'll sound the *noisemaker* when you need their attention and you'll wait for all of them to look at you without talking before you continue.

Before you begin the lesson, ask kids about last week's "Table Talk" discussions. Use questions such as "How were you able to identify conflict-causing situations?" and "How were you able to understand your own anger and avoid conflict because of it?" However, be careful not to alienate students whose families chose not to use "Table Talk."

ATTENTION GRABBER

LEARNING LAB

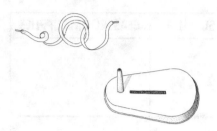

ALL TIED UP

(up to 10 minutes)

Pick up one of the *neon shoelaces,* and say: **Think about a time you were so angry with someone that you wouldn't forgive him or her. Tell us about it.** Have volunteers briefly tell their stories. As each story is told, tie a knot in the *neon shoelace.* Space out the knots so you can get six or eight on the lace. When you've got six or eight knots, hold up the knotted lace and ask:

◆ **How useful is this shoelace for lacing up a shoe as it is?**

◆ **How is the knotted shoelace like the way our lives get knotted up when we refuse to forgive?**

Say: **Today we're going to be looking at forgiveness and how we can forgive others even when it's hard.** ☞ **God wants us to forgive others as he's forgiven us.**

Save the *neon shoelaces* for use in later lessons.

THE **POINT**

BIBLE EXPLORATION AND APPLICATION

LEARNING LAB

DISAPPEARING UNFORGIVENESS

(up to 12 minutes)

Have kids form pairs, and give each student a sheet of paper. Say: **In your pairs, take turns telling each other about a time you didn't forgive someone. After you tell your situation, raise your hand and I'll place a few drops of ink on your paper to represent that situation.**

Walk around to all the pairs and place several drops of *disappearing ink* on the paper (the ink will form a small bubble on the paper) and instruct kids not to touch the ink. Ask:

◆ **What was it like thinking about your situation?**

◆ **How has the ink blobs on your paper damaged your once-clean paper?**

◆ **How are the ink marks like the damage caused to relationships by a person unwilling to forgive?**

◆ **How would you feel if you would've forgiven the person in your situation?**

Say: **Let's do that now. The ink bubble represents the unforgiven person. Place your finger in the ink bubble and say, "I forgive you" while gently rubbing the ink bubble with your finger.**

When everyone's ink has disappeared, ask:

◆ **What was it like seeing your ink disappear?**

◆ **How does it feel to forgive a person you previously didn't forgive?**

Give pairs each a Bible and have them read **Matthew 6:12-15.** Ask:

◆ **Why do you think God wants us to forgive?**

◆ **What does this passage say will happen if we forgive others?**

◆ **How would the situation with the unforgiven person have turned out better in real life if you had applied Matthew 6:14?**

Hold up one of the papers and say: **Just as using _disappearing ink_ on this paper left it undamaged, forgiving others helps us restore damaged relationships.** ☞ **God wants us to forgive others as he's forgiven us, even when it's hard.**

Return the _disappearing ink_ to the Learning Lab for future use.

TEACHER TIP

It's important to say The Point just as it's written in each activity. Repeating The Point over and over will help kids remember it and apply it to their lives.

☜ THE **POINT**

▊ **LIKE GOD FORGIVES**

(up to 15 minutes)

Form groups of four or five. Say: **Turn to Matthew 18:23-35 and take turns reading the verses. Then think of a modern-day skit your group can act out to illustrate the passage.** Have each group read through **Matthew 18:21-35** and put together a modern story to act out based on this passage. Encourage kids to be creative. While kids are working on their skits, go from group to group giving help as necessary. Some groups may not need any help; others may need lots. They may need help thinking of modern situations. If so, give them these suggestions:

◆ a big brother and a little brother (or big sister and little sister);

◆ a parent and a child;

◆ a teacher and a student; or

◆ a coach and a team captain.

When the groups are ready, have them present their skits.

▬ **BIBLE** INSIGHT

When Jesus called him to be an apostle, Matthew was a tax collector, one of the most despised members of society. Worse, he was a Jewish tax collector who collected revenue for the Roman government. He was therefore considered a traitor to his people, who would have had a tough time forgiving him. Perhaps due to this, Matthew felt a personal connection to the parable of the unmerciful servant, as it is only found in Matthew's Gospel (Matthew 18:23-35). The fact that Jesus chose him as one of the twelve is a practical application of the forgiveness Jesus taught about in the parable.

THE **POINT**

─**KEY VERSE** *CONNECTION*

"So in everything, do to others what you would have them do to you" (Matthew 7:12a).

Fifth- and sixth-graders are at a bewildering and volatile age. Their emotions change quickly and often, and feelings are easily bruised. The Key Verse can help kids find a way to forgive others and to ask for forgiveness themselves.

THE **POINT**

TEACHER TIP

Encourage active participation as students share by following up kids' answers with questions such as "What did you mean by that?" and "Can you tell me more?"

THE **POINT**

When the skits are finished, ask:

◆ **What's something new you learned about forgiving others from the Bible passage and the skits?**

Say: **God wants us to forgive others as he's forgiven us. And he's always willing to forgive us. The power to forgive comes from God. He's always ready to help us forgive. Let's see how we can start forgiving others right now.**

OBEY THE PARABLE

(up to 13 minutes)

Say: **Open your Bibles to Matthew 18 again.** Have a volunteer read **Matthew 18:21-22** while the others follow along. Ask:

◆ **Why do you think it's important to Jesus that we keep forgiving people?**

Say: **Forgiving people each time they hurt us takes patience. It's not easy. But** **God wants us to forgive others as he's forgiven us.**

Give kids paper and pens or pencils. Tell kids to write their own parables, based on the lesson of **Matthew 18:21-22,** that describe real-life situations in which they need to forgive others. For example, kids might write about a friend at school who has made them angry or about an argument with a parent that turned out poorly. If kids can't think of any present situation in which they need to forgive someone, have them write about a time in the past when they forgave someone.

When kids are finished, have them form trios to share their parables. Then have trios discuss these questions:

◆ **Have you actually forgiven in real life the person you wrote about in your story? Why or why not?**

◆ **Why is forgiving others hard sometimes?**

◆ **Why is it always best for us to forgive the people who hurt us?**

After the discussion, have several volunteers share what they discussed in their trios. Then say: **Forgiving others is hard sometimes, but** **God wants us to forgive others as he's forgiven us. Let's close today by discovering why it's so important for us to forgive others.**

Christian education extends beyond the classroom into the home. Photocopy the "Table Talk" handout (p. 70) for this week, and send it home with your kids. Encourage kids and parents to use the handout to spark meaningful discussion on this week's topic. Follow up next week by asking kids how their discussions with their families went.

CLOSING

AROMA OF FORGIVENESS

(up to 10 minutes)

Have kids form a circle and pinch their noses shut with their hands. Open the *package of spices* and then walk around the circle and ask kids to try to smell the spices without unpinching their noses. Once everyone has tried to smell the spices, ask:

◆ **How did it feel to try to smell the spices?**

◆ **How is trying to smell the spices with your nose pinched shut like trying to live with unforgiveness in your heart?**

Walk around the circle with the spices again. This time, let kids rub their fingers in the spices and then smell the aroma on their fingertips. Once everyone has smelled the spices, ask:

◆ **How is your attempt to smell the spices this time different from your first attempt?**

◆ **How is the difference between these two attempts like the difference forgiveness makes in our lives?**

Say: ☞ **God wants us to forgive others as he's forgiven us because he knows our lives will never be rich and full of "spice" as long as we hold on to unforgiveness in our hearts. Let's close today by thanking God for his forgiveness and for the privilege of forgiving others.**

Close your class with prayer, thanking God for forgiving us and asking him to help us forgive others.

LEARNING LAB

 THE **POINT**

Discussion Starters

◉ ◆ Why do you think Jesus commanded us to forgive others?

◆ How is unforgiveness like a prison? How is it different?

Family Building

*For Kids Only: Make a point to forgive anyone you've been unable to forgive. Ask God to give you the strength to do this.

*For Parents Only: Take a drive to a quiet place. Ask God to show you any unforgiveness you're holding on to. Then ask God to help you forgive. Support the offender in an appropriate way by either praying for, calling, or visiting him or her.

*For the Family: Have a "New Start" celebration for your family. On the night before the celebration, spend time as a family confessing the sins you have committed against each other, forgiving each other, and asking God for forgiveness. (As an alternative to confessing sins to each other, spend quiet time with God confessing any sins). On the day of your celebration, have a feast to celebrate your new start in a new year of God's forgiveness.

Something to Think About

◉ "How can I forgive my parents for getting a divorce when I'll have to deal with it for the rest of my life?" "How can I forgive my friend for back-stabbing me when he hasn't even said he was sorry?" "Sue punched me right in the nose, and I'm supposed to say that it was OK. I don't think I can ever forgive her."

We all know that we should forgive, but sometimes it's just so hard. Forgiveness isn't saying something was OK when it wasn't OK. Forgiveness isn't about pretending that a person never did anything wrong. Forgiveness is about giving up your right to revenge. It's about letting go of your bitterness and hate toward another person. When Jesus told us to forgive others, he wasn't telling us to ignore our feelings or close our eyes to our hurt. Jesus was telling us to acknowledge our feelings and to give our hurt to him. It's hard to forgive others, but we have to do it. When we don't forgive, we are just hurting ourselves.

"For if you forgive men when they sin against you, your heavenly Father will also forgive you. But if you do not forgive men their sins, your Father will not forgive your sins"

(Matthew 6:14-15).

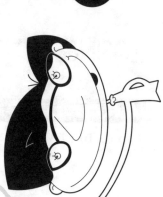

Table Talk

Group's hands-On BiBLE curriculum

Forgiving Others, Week 6

Permission to photocopy this handout from Group's Hands-On Bible Curriculum™ for Grades 5 and 6 granted for local church use. Copyright © Group Publishing, Inc., P.O. Box 481, Loveland, CO 80539.

BETWEEN GUYS AND GIRLS

THE POINT

☞ **God helps guys and girls develop good friendships.**

THE BIBLE BASIS

Ephesians 5:1-5

Be imitators of God, therefore, as dearly loved children and live a life of love, just as Christ loved us and gave himself up for us as a fragrant offering and sacrifice to God.

But among you there must not be even a hint of sexual immorality, or of any kind of impurity, or of greed, because these are improper for God's holy people. Nor should there be obscenity, foolish talk or coarse joking, which are out of place, but rather thanksgiving. For of this you can be sure: No immoral, impure or greedy person—such a man is an idolater—has any inheritance in the kingdom of Christ and of God.

KEY VERSE
for Lessons 5–9

"So in everything, do to others what you would have them do to you."

(Matthew 7:12a)

Dishonesty, crime, and immorality may abound now, but they were certainly not unheard of in Bible times. In this passage, Paul tells his readers that they're to be different from the people around them. Instead of being selfish pleasure-seekers, they are to be caring, sacrificing, God-pleasing people.

Your kids have grown up in a society obsessed with self and pleasure. And left in the dust are people who have been used and hurt by people of the opposite sex who are on the pleasure track. Kids have likely already felt the hurt of other people's selfishness and may be tending toward a selfish lifestyle themselves.

Use this lesson to help your kids see that caring relationships with members of the opposite sex are possible and are what God, as our loving heavenly Father, wants for us.

GETTING THE POINT

Students will
- ◆ examine feelings toward the opposite sex,
- ◆ consider how God wants them to treat members of the opposite sex, and
- ◆ commit to treating members of the opposite sex in a caring and unselfish way.

THIS LESSON AT A GLANCE

Before the lesson, collect the necessary items from the Learning Lab for the activities you plan to use. Refer to the pictures in the margin to see what each item looks like.

SECTION	MINUTES	WHAT STUDENTS WILL DO	LEARNING LAB SUPPLIES	CLASSROOM SUPPLIES
ATTENTION GRABBER	up to 10	**To Ask**—Choose from a list of questions to ask people of the opposite sex.		"To Ask or Not to Ask" handouts (p. 78)
BIBLE EXPLORATION AND APPLICATION	up to 15	**Gender Towers**—Compete with the opposite sex to build a tower while their hands are tied together and then discuss Ephesians 5:1-2.	Neon shoelaces, plastic rings	Bibles, shoelaces or string
	up to 15	**Scripture Hunt**—Read Ephesians 5:3-5 and then toss a ball as they suggest actions that are displeasing or pleasing to God.	Inflatable eyeball	Bibles, chalkboard and chalk or newsprint and marker
	up to 13	**Commitment Rings**—Read Ephesians 5:1-2 and give one another rings symbolic of a commitment.	Plastic rings	Bibles
CLOSING	up to 7	**Friends Forever**—Sing a song celebrating the gift of friendship.	Cassette: "Friends," "Lyrics Poster"	Cassette player
		Remember to make photocopies of the "Table Talk" handout (p. 79) to send home with your kids. "Table Talk" is a valuable tool for helping fifth- and sixth-graders talk with their parents about what they're learning in class.		

THE LESSON

When kids arrive, remind them that you'll sound the *noisemaker* when you need their attention and you'll wait for all of them to look at you without talking before you continue.

Before you begin the lesson, ask kids about last week's "Table Talk" discussions. Use questions such as "How were you able to forgive someone?" and "How did your family members forgive one another?" However, be careful not to alienate students whose families chose not to use "Table Talk."

ATTENTION GRABBER

[handwritten: Friendships · opposite sex — Like EAch other — girl FRIEND Boy FRIEND]

[handwritten: RPAD Ephesian — 5 (1-5)]

TO ASK

(up to 10 minutes)

[handwritten: ASK — me Question EAch — Boy GIRL — GIRL - Boy]

Pair kids up in mixed-gender pairs. If you have unequal numbers of girls and guys, form the smallest groups you can with at least one guy and one girl in each group.

Give kids each a photocopy of the "To Ask or Not to Ask" handout (p. 78). In their pairs or groups, have kids each choose three of the questions from the handout to ask each opposite-sex partner. Give kids about four minutes to discuss the questions.

Then have each group pair up with another group to discuss the following questions. After each question, have volunteers report how their groups answered the question and why.

Ask:

◆ **How did it feel to ask these questions? Explain.** *[handwritten: To the opposite sex]*

◆ **How is this like you sometimes feel when you're trying to speak with someone of your age of the opposite sex?**

Say: **Sometimes it's hard to begin talking with people of the opposite sex, but once we get past the awkwardness, it's usually not so bad. In fact,**  **God helps guys and girls develop good friendships. That's what we're going to be talking about today.**

LEARNING LAB

KEY VERSE CONNECTION

"So in everything, do to others what you would have them do to you" (Matthew 7:12a).

Forming friendships with the opposite sex can be a harrowing experience for the kids in your class. Despite exposure to graphic advertisements, movies, and music, most kids still enter this phase of development with sweaty palms and faltering voices. Use the Key Verse to help kids realize that honesty and kindness are essential to successful relationships.

☜ THE POINT

BIBLE EXPLORATION AND APPLICATION

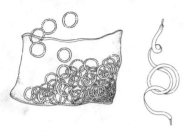

GENDER TOWERS

(up to 15 minutes)

Form mixed-gender groups of six or fewer, making the proportion of guys and girls as equal as possible. Have members of each group form a circle and arrange themselves so that each of the guys is between two girls. Then have everyone kneel on the floor. Ask kids to remove their shoelaces from their shoes or provide enough two-foot sections of string and *neon shoelaces* so each person has a strand. With help from their group members, have group members each tie their left hands to the right hands of the people next to them.

Divide the *plastic rings* into equal numbers for each group, and place them in the center of each group. Then say: **We're going to see how guys and girls can cooperate with each other in your group. On "go," the guys in your group will take turns stacking the *plastic rings* on top of each other to create a tower. At the same time, the girls will take turns stacking the rings to make a separate tower of their own. You have one minute. Go!**

Start the contest and then call time after one minute. While kids' hands remain tied together, have groups discuss these questions:

◆ **What's your reaction to this activity?**

◆ **What was it like to try to build your own tower while being tied to someone who was also trying to build his or her own tower?**

◆ **How did being tied to one another help or hurt your ability to cooperate with each other?**

◆ **How would the activity have been different if everyone in your group was trying to build the same tower?**

◆ **How is the way you were forced to cooperate with each other like the way you feel forced to cooperate with members of the opposite sex?**

◆ **How does it feel right now to remain tied to someone of the opposite sex?**

◆ **What does this activity teach us about the problems of cooperating with people of the opposite sex?**

◆ **How could this activity help us see how God wants us to treat members of the opposite sex?**

Ask kids to share what they discovered in their small-group

discussions. Then let kids untie their hands. Say: **The Bible tells us how to treat others, including people of the opposite sex.**

Have a volunteer in each group read **Ephesians 5:1-2** aloud as the other group members follow along. Have kids take turns answering the following questions in their groups. Ask:

◆ **What made Jesus' life a "life of love"?**

◆ **What could make our lives a bit more like Jesus' life of love?**

Say: **God wants us to be like Jesus. Jesus cared about people, no matter if they were men or women or children.** **God helps guys and girls develop good friendships. Learning ways to cooperate with each other is one way we can follow God's will. But there are many other ways to develop solid friendships between guys and girls. Let's brainstorm ways to have caring attitudes toward each other.**

Gather the Learning Lab items for future use.

SCRIPTURE HUNT

(up to 15 minutes) *NEWS PRINT*

Have a volunteer read aloud **Ephesians 5:3-5** as others follow along. Write the following words on the left side of the chalkboard or newsprint: "sexual immorality," "impurity," "greed," "obscenity," "foolish talk," and "coarse joking."

Hold up the *inflatable eyeball,* and say: **All these things that are mentioned in today's passage are things that we *see* happening around us. But what do they mean in our lives today? What do we see in our society that falls into these categories? Raise your hand as you think of an example.**

Toss the *inflatable eyeball* to someone with a raised hand. That person must give an answer and then toss the ball to someone of the opposite sex who then must say how that action is displeasing to God or how it hurts someone else. For example, if the first person says "lying," the second person might say, "This makes God upset because he wants us to be honest." List the action, such as lying, on the chalkboard or newsprint right under the other words.

Then have the person holding the *inflatable eyeball* toss it to someone of the opposite sex who has his or her hand raised. Continue this until you have about eight negative things listed on your chalkboard or newsprint.

Have each student take a turn answering the following question. If your class is larger than ten, form smaller groups

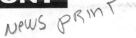
THE **POINT**

LEARNING LAB

BIBLE INSIGHT

Paul had his work cut out for him to preach Christianity to the Ephesians. Ephesus was not only a key Mediterranean city but a stronghold of pagan religion with immoral practices, including "worship" with temple prostitutes. In fact, the pagan temple was the crux of Ephesus' economic prosperity. The pagan environment made it important for Paul to warn Christians to avoid the immorality commonly practiced by the people.

of no more than five to answer and discuss this question and then have those groups report to the whole class what they talked about. Ask:

◆ **How does seeing some of these negative things hurt your relationships with the opposite sex?** Girls or Boys

◆ **How can we avoid these negative things in our relationships with the opposite sex?**

Now write the following words on the other side of the chalkboard or newsprint: "acting like God," "being loving," and "thanking God." This time, toss the *inflatable eyeball* to someone in the group, and ask kids for actions that are right, such as "helping friends in need" or "telling the truth." Once again, list these on the newsprint or chalkboard under the other positive actions.

When you have a list of at least eight positive actions, put the *inflatable eyeball* away for use in later lessons, and ask:

◆ **How can God help us "see" these positive actions?**

◆ **How can we show more of these positive actions in our relationships with the opposite sex?**

◆ **How will this help your relationships?**

Say: **God wants us to have a caring attitude toward everyone, even kids of the opposite sex. If we work on the actions we've talked about here, we can discover how God helps guys and girls develop good friendships.**

TEACHER TIP

It's important to say The Point just as it's written in each activity. Repeating The Point over and over will help kids remember it and apply it to their lives.

THE **POINT**

LEARNING LAB

COMMITMENT RINGS

(up to 13 minutes)

Say: **As we think about developing friendships with the opposite sex, let's turn back to our first passage from Ephesians.** Have a volunteer read aloud **Ephesians 5:1-2** as other students follow along.

Say: **A ring is a symbol of a covenant—an agreement or contract. Today we're going to use these *plastic rings* as symbols of a covenant among all of us in the class. If you're willing to, I'd like each of you to agree in this covenant to treat all members of the opposite sex in an unselfish way—the way God would want you to.**

Give each student one *plastic ring* to wear on one of his or her fingers. Save the rest of the rings for use in later lessons.

Say: **Now that you're wearing a ring of commitment, go up to three members of the opposite sex and tell each of them one thing you appreciate about him or her. For example, you might tell someone you appreciate how**

he or she is a good listener.

Allow time for kids to give affirmations to each other. Then ask:

◆ **What was it like giving compliments? receiving them?**

◆ **How can having friends of the opposite sex help you?**

Say:  **God helps guys and girls develop good friendships, and we've taken some positive steps toward doing that today.**

 THE **POINT**

TABLE TALK

Christian education extends beyond the classroom into the home. Photocopy the "Table Talk" handout (p. 79) for this week, and send it home with your kids. Encourage kids and parents to use the handout to spark meaningful discussion on this week's topic. Follow up next week by asking kids how their discussions with their families went.

CLOSING

FRIENDS FOREVER

(up to 7 minutes)

Say: **It's not always easy to treat others the way we should. Peer pressure and natural human desires can make us selfish. But God can help us overcome those pressures and desires.**  **God helps guys and girls develop good friendships. And if we rely on God to help us, our friendships can last a lifetime.**

Sing "Friends" with the *cassette tape* to close your session. You'll find the words printed on a "Lyrics Poster" in the Learning Lab. Return the *cassette tape* and the "Lyrics Poster" to the Learning Lab.

Wrap up your class with prayer. Have the guys start by praying for the girls in your class, asking God to bless them and to help the guys in the group treat them with kindness and respect the way God wants them to. Then have girls pray something similar for the guys in your group.

LEARNING LAB

To Ask or Not to Ask

What do you like least about school? What do you like most?

What's your favorite thing to do in your spare time?

Who's your biggest hero? Why?

What do you think you'll do for a living when you get older?

Where is your favorite spot in the world? Why?

If you could change one thing about yourself, what would it be?

Discussion Starters

- What differences (besides the obvious physical differences) are there between boys and girls?
- How can you value those differences in relating to the opposite sex?
- How do your personal stereotypes affect the way you relate to the opposite sex?

Family Building

*For Kids Only: Ask your parents one question you've always wanted to know about the opposite sex.

*For Parents Only: Open up a frank discussion to help your preteen relate to the opposite sex. Explore topics about sexuality, friendships, and other developmental issues. Helping your child navigate the stormy seas of early adolescence will build trust between you and your child.

*For the Family: Go through a magazine designed for boys and a magazine designed for girls. As a family, point out the false assumptions each magazine has about boys, girls, and relationships between the two.

Something to Think About

Make a copy of this page for each member of your family. Have each family member mark his or her answers and then compare your answers as a family.

Take a look at the gender stereotypes as seen by the various members of your family by answering which of the following activities are done mostly by boys, mostly by girls, or done about the same amount by both:

Activity	Mostly done by girls	Mostly done by boys	About the same for boys and girls
playing soccer			
lying			
running track			
burping			
problem solving			
doing well in English			
getting in trouble			
talking			
gossiping			
laughing			
dancing			
doing well in math			
playing football			
crying			
bragging			
fighting			
playing an instrument			
flirting			

"So God created man in his own image, in the image of God he created him; male and female he created them"
(Genesis 1:27).

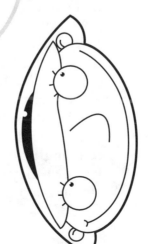

LESSON 8

STANDING STRONG

THE POINT

☞ **God will honor us for standing strong.**

KEY *VERSE*
for Lessons 5–9

"So in everything, do to others what you would have them do to you."

(Matthew 7:12a)

THE BIBLE BASIS
Numbers 14:20-24 *5-9*

> The Lord replied, "I have forgiven them, as you asked. Nevertheless, as surely as I live and as surely as the glory of the Lord fills the whole earth, not one of the men who saw my glory and the miraculous signs I performed in Egypt and in the desert but who disobeyed me and tested me ten times—not one of them will ever see the land I promised on oath to their forefathers. No one who has treated me with contempt will ever see it. But because my servant Caleb has a different spirit and follows me wholeheartedly, I will bring him into the land he went to, and his descendants will inherit it."

The people of Israel had come to the edge of the Promised Land. Spies came back with reports of a paradise—the land God had prepared for them. But most of the spies also reported terror at the size of the people in the land. And they convinced the Israelites they couldn't possibly win. God punished them for their faithlessness by making them wander in the desert for forty years.

But two spies stood up against the rest. Caleb and Joshua had confidence that God would make a difference if they followed him. And in the end, he did. Of the twelve spies, only Caleb and Joshua were allowed to live long enough to see the Promised Land.

Kids today <u>face pressures</u> to do wrong things at earlier and earlier ages. And in many cases, they're not prepared to handle the pressure.

Use this lesson to help your kids see the importance of standing up against pressures to do wrong. And help them see that they've got powerful backing when they do stand strong against those pressures.

Other Scriptures used in this lesson are **Numbers 14:5-9, 26-35** and **2 Thessalonians 2:15–3:3.**

GETTING THE POINT

Students will
◆ examine how hard it can be to take a stand,
◆ discuss pressures they feel, and
◆ learn to seek help when they feel pressured.

THIS LESSON AT A GLANCE

Before the lesson, collect the necessary items from the Learning Lab for the activities you plan to use. Refer to the pictures in the margin to see what each item looks like.

SECTION	MINUTES	WHAT STUDENTS WILL DO	LEARNING LAB SUPPLIES	CLASSROOM SUPPLIES
ATTENTION GRABBER	up to 11	**Truth Quest**—Search for an object while looking through a prism scope.	Prism scopes, inflatable eyeball	
BIBLE EXPLORATION AND APPLICATION	up to 13	**Making a Way**—Search for the object again with the addition of protectors and guides and then discuss Numbers 14:5-9, 20-24.	Prism scopes, inflatable eyeball	Bibles
	up to 13	**Standing-Strong Test**—Try to stand perfectly still while others try to distract them and then discuss 2 Thessalonians 2:15–3:3.	All Learning Lab items	Bibles
	up to 13	**The Pressures I Face**—Choose Learning Lab items that represent pressures they feel in life, discuss how to combat those pressures, and discuss Numbers 14:26-35.	All Learning Lab items	Bibles, newsprint, tape, markers
CLOSING	up to 10	**United We Stand**—Experience starting to fall when a group member is pulled away, and discuss how they can help each other stand strong.		

Remember to make photocopies of the "Table Talk" handout (p. 88) to send home with your kids. "Table Talk" is a valuable tool for helping fifth- and sixth-graders talk with their parents about what they're learning in class.

THE LESSON ▬▬▬

When kids arrive, remind them that you'll sound the *noisemaker* when you need their attention and you'll wait for all of them to look at you without talking before you continue.

Before you begin the lesson, ask kids about last week's "Table Talk" discussions. Use questions such as "What were you able to learn about the opposite sex?" and "What false assumptions about the opposite sex were you able to discern?" However, be careful not to alienate students whose families chose not to use "Table Talk."

ATTENTION GRABBER ▬▬▬

LEARNING LAB

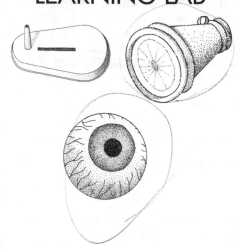

TRUTH QUEST

(up to 11 minutes)

Form two teams, and have each team choose a Captain. Give one team Captain two *prism scopes* and then say: **In a moment, I'm going to ask this team Captain to look through the *prism scopes* and go on a quest to find the All-Seeing Eye of Truth** (hold up the *inflatable eyeball)* **that I have placed somewhere in the room.**

Then, in the presence of the class, say to the Captain: **At no time should anyone from your group help you find the Eye of Truth. However, the members of the other group can do all they want to distract you from your quest except touch you. For example, they can stand in your way, wave their arms in front of your *prism scopes,* or try to lure you away from the object you're searching for.**

Say to the class: **Once the first Captain has tried to locate the Eye of Truth, we'll switch roles and give the other team Captain a chance.**

Have the Captains close their eyes. Set out the *inflatable eyeball* in one of the corners of the room and then lead one of the Captains to the front of the room. Make sure the Captain's eyes remain closed. Have the team Captain begin the quest. Make sure he or she looks through the *prism scopes* at all times. Encourage the members of the opposing team to do all they can to distract the Captain short of touching him or her.

After a few minutes, or when the *inflatable eyeball* is found, have the other team's Captain give it a try. (If you have extra time, let a few other team members try it as well.)

TEACHER TIP

Encourage active participation in the discussion by following up kids' answers with questions such as "What did you mean by that?" and "Can you tell me more?"

Then gather everyone together and collect the *prism scopes* and *inflatable eyeball* for later use. Ask:

◆ **What was it like to look for the Eye of Truth while using the *prism scopes* and being distracted by the opposing team members?**

◆ **How is that like trying to follow God's teachings in the midst of the daily pressures of life?**

◆ **How does the influence of others' ideas of the truth make following God difficult?**

◆ **What was it like to try to distract the team Captains from their quest?**

◆ **How is that like the way Satan tries to distract us from doing what's right?**

Say: **Sometimes it's really hard to do what's right when others want us to do something that's wrong. But** **God will honor us for standing strong. And today we're going to take a look at how we can do that.**

BIBLE EXPLORATION AND APPLICATION

MAKING A WAY

(up to 13 minutes)

LEARNING LAB

Have kids return to their teams, and have one of the teams choose a new team Captain. Once again, have the Captain close his or her eyes while you place the *inflatable eyeball* somewhere in the room. This time, however, hide the *inflatable eyeball* so it isn't plainly visible.

Lead the team Captain to the front of the room, and give him or her the two *prism scopes.* As before, have the Captain search for the *inflatable eyeball* using the *prism scopes,* and allow the opposing team members to try to distract him or her from the quest. But this time, encourage the Captain's teammates to help him or her in any way they can. For example, they can point to where the eyeball is hidden or tell the Captain which direction to go to reach it.

After the team Captain has found the eyeball, gather everyone together and ask:

◆ **Was it easy to find the *inflatable eyeball?* Why or why not?**

◆ **How did the Captain's teammates help him or her find it?**

◆ **How is that like the help we sometimes get in standing against pressures to do wrong?**

◆ **What are specific ways our Christian friends can help us stand against pressures to do wrong?**

◆ **What are ways God can help us stand against pressures to do wrong?**

◆ **Does it take courage to stand strong in doing what's right? Why or why not?**

Say: **Sometimes it takes courage to stand strong. Let's look at someone in the Bible who had that courage.** Have kids find partners and read **Numbers 14:5-9, 20-24** together. Have them answer the following questions. Ask:

◆ **What did Caleb do to get help from God?**

◆ **How can we get the kind of help from God that Caleb got?**

Have volunteers share their answers with the rest of the group.

Say: **Joshua and Caleb didn't "just say no" to the pressure to go along with the others. They enthusiastically disagreed with the other spies. And they trusted in God. Sometimes we have to be creative in standing up against pressures to do wrong. Sometimes we have to give answers that are more difficult than yes or no. And we always need to remember that God is our support.**

☞ **God will honor us for standing strong. Let's explore the kinds of pressures you face each day.**

Collect the *prism scopes* and *inflatable eyeball* for later use.

▬ BIBLE *INSIGHT*

Caleb finally did enter the Promised Land, just as God promised. He was appointed to the commission created by Moses to assign allotments to the tribes of Israel. Caleb represented Judah on the commission. He was eighty-five years old when Joshua gave him the city of Hebron.

Read— passage in Bible Button

THE **POINT** ☞

LEARNING LAB

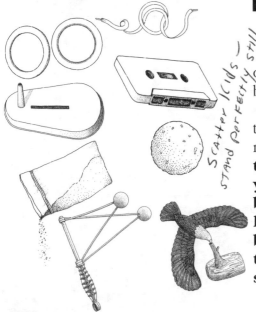

Scatter kids / stand perfectly still

STANDING-STRONG TEST 📖

(up to 13 minutes)

Have kids remain in their two teams. Scatter the members of one team all over the room and instruct them to "stand strong" by standing perfectly still—absolutely no movement is allowed.

While the first team "stands strong," gather the second team together and distribute the Learning Lab items among the team members. Say: **Use these Learning Lab items to try to get the members of the other team to move. For example, you can use the *noisemakers* to try to startle them from behind, or you can tape the *inflatable eyeball* to your head to try to make them laugh. Any movement beyond a blink counts. The only catch is that you may not touch them or throw any Learning Lab item at them. Each person you get to move must go stand against the wall.**

When kids understand the instructions, start the game. Continue for three or four minutes, or until all the "standing strong" kids have moved. Then have teams switch roles and repeat the activity. Once both groups have tried to "stand strong" against pressures of the other team, have kids gather in groups of four to discuss these questions:

◆ **What was hard about this game?**

◆ **How was trying to "stand strong" against the opposing team's efforts like trying to stand strong for God in real life?**

◆ **Do you think it's possible to always stand strong for God in real life? Why or why not?**

Say: **We all need help in standing strong—especially when it's hard, like it was in this game. The Bible tells us where we can go for that help.**

Have the groups sit on the floor where they are and look up **2 Thessalonians 2:15–3:3.** Have a volunteer in each group read the passage while the others follow along. Then have the groups discuss the following questions. Ask:

◆ **What does this passage say about standing strong for God?** Don't Judge - Have Faith

◆ **According to this passage, what are ways God can help us stand strong?** pray - grace

◆ **What are ways we can help each other?** - Stand up for Each other - Remind each other about pray

Have volunteers share their discoveries with the rest of the class. Then say: **God knows that it's hard to do right when we're pressured to do wrong. But he promises to give us strength and to encourage us. He won't leave us alone.**  **God will honor us for standing strong against pressures to do wrong—even the "giant" pressures we face.**

Collect the Learning Lab items for use in later lessons.

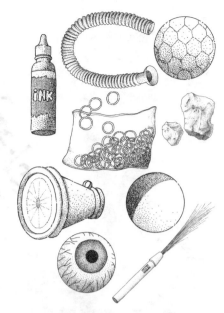

KEY VERSE
CONNECTION

"So in everything, do to others what you would have them do to you" (Matthew 7:12a).

Perhaps never before have kids been faced with such powerful pressure to slip away from God's path for their lives. Show kids that following this Key Verse can provide a powerful tool in the struggle to stand strong.

🖎 THE **POINT**

THE PRESSURES I FACE

📖

(up to 13 minutes)

Have kids stay in their groups of four or fewer. Set out all the Learning Lab items in the center of the room. Then have each person choose one Learning Lab item to represent a specific pressure he or she faces in real life. (If more than one person chooses the same Learning Lab item, just have kids take turns holding the item.) Once kids have each chosen an item, have them take turns showing the item to their group members and explaining what specific real-life pressure it represents. For

LEARNING LAB

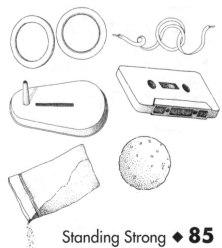

example, someone might say the *inflatable eyeball* represents the constant pressure that he or she feels from parents to be the best. Or someone might choose a *noisemaker,* saying it represents the constant badgering from friends to drink or take drugs.

While kids share, tape a sheet of newsprint to the wall and title it "Real-Life Pressures." When groups finish sharing, have them call out the pressures they named in their groups. List kids' responses on the newsprint. Be sure to keep each group's responses separate on the newsprint.

When all the groups have shared, say: **Keep these pressures we just wrote in mind as we read this next passage.** In their groups, have group members read together through **Numbers 14:26-35** and answer the following questions. Ask:

◆ **How did the actions of some of the Israelites hurt the whole community?**

◆ **How is that like the actions of those who try to influence you to not follow God?**

◆ **How did Joshua and Caleb "stand strong" for God?**

◆ **Who helps you "stand strong" for God?**

◆ **Why do you think God rewarded Joshua and Caleb?**

◆ **What difference can following God make in our lives?**

Have groups share with the class how they responded to the last question.

Then say: **Now that we've shared some of the pressures we face, let's devise practical ways we can combat those real-life pressures and "stand strong" for God.**

Assign each group one of the other groups' lists of pressures. Then, in their groups, have kids work together to come up with one way to combat each of the pressures the other group named. For example, kids might combat the pressure from friends to do drugs by finding new friends. Or kids might combat the pressure from parents to be the best by telling their parents about their feelings. If kids have trouble coming up with ideas, encourage them to read the Scriptures covered in the lesson one more time and see if they can find any ideas there.

When groups are ready, have them take turns presenting their real-life pressures and their practical advice for combating those pressures. As kids share their insights, use a marker to list kids' ideas next to the appropriate pressures on the newsprint.

Say: **When we let God help us, the pressures that come at us are much easier to face than they are when we face them alone. We can stand against pressures. And** ☞ **God will honor us for standing strong against pressures to do wrong.**

THE **POINT** ☞

Leave the newsprint on your classroom wall to remind kids that God will help them stand against pressures to do wrong.

Collect the Learning Lab items for later use.

TABLE TALK

Christian education extends beyond the classroom into the home. Photocopy the "Table Talk" handout (p. 88) for this week, and send it home with your kids. Encourage kids and parents to use the handout to spark meaningful discussion on this week's topic. Follow up next week by asking kids how their discussions with their families went.

CLOSING

UNITED WE STAND

(up to 10 minutes)

Form circles of three. Group guys and girls in separate circles as much as possible. Have kids in each group stand facing each other and lean their heads in until their foreheads touch. Then have kids take small steps backward until they are supporting themselves by leaning against the other kids' foreheads. Let kids remain this way for a few seconds. Then ask:

◆ **What would happen if one or more of you suddenly stepped back quickly?**

Go around to each group, grasp the shoulders of one student, and pull him or her backward out of the circle. Pull quickly, but don't pull so hard that kids will risk injury.

After kids in each group have nearly fallen down, say: **There's an old saying that says, "United we stand; divided we fall." And there's a lot of truth to that saying.**

☞ **God will honor us for standing strong. But we don't have to stand alone. We can support each other in standing against pressures, just as we supported each other in our circles.**

Lead kids in a prayer to thank God for helping them stand strong. If your kids are comfortable with it, have them pray together in their circles before wrapping up your session.

 **THE POINT**

Discussion Starters

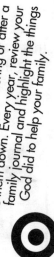

- ◆ What are some of the most difficult things you have had to go through?
- ◆ If you were Sage, how could God help you stand strong?
- ◆ How does God help us stand strong in difficult times?

Family Building

*For Kids Only: Help someone you know who is going through a difficult time stand strong by spending time and praying with him or her.

*For Parents Only: To help your family stand strong during difficult times, get in touch with the trials and pain of others. Take your family to a hospice center, the children's ward of a hospital, or visiting others who are hurting. Make sure you talk with your children about their experiences and impressions.

*For the Family: Start a family journal. In your journal, record the trials your family goes through and the blessings God brings. If God gives you any special insights during or after a trial, write them down. Every year, review your family journal and highlight the things God did to help your family.

Something to Think About

Mr. Volkman saw smoke coming from the direction of his campsite. He raced back to find that his camper was on fire and his daughter, Sage, was still sleeping inside! Mr. Volkman kicked down the door and pulled his daughter out. Her sleeping bag was melting, and she was on fire.

At six years old, Sage lost both hands, an ear, and her nose in the fire. The doctors weren't sure if Sage would even survive. Her bandages were changed more than once every day, and she was given hot baths for the two months she was in the hospital. The pain was so intense, she had to be given powerful painkillers every time she was even touched.

Sage never gave up hope. After she was released from the hospital, Sage went through rehabilitation, she got an artificial hand, and she had a series of operations to restore her skin. Sage is still disfigured and people stare at her when they see her for the first time. But Sage keeps going. "If people stare or run away, that's their problem, not mine," says Sage.

Sage will still need more operations as she grows older, but she has hope for the future. In fact, she wants to be a doctor. With her perseverance and determination, she'll be able to follow her dreams.

(from *Kid Heroes* by Neal Shusterman)

"But we also rejoice in our sufferings, because we know that suffering produces perseverance; perseverance, character; and character, hope"

(Romans 5:3b-4).

Table Talk

Group's
hands·On
BiBLE
curriculum

Standing Strong, Week 8

BUILDING OTHERS UP

THE POINT

☞ **God wants us to build people up.**

THE BIBLE BASIS

1 Thessalonians 5:4-11

> But you, brothers, are not in darkness so that this day should surprise you like a thief. You are all sons of the light and sons of the day. We do not belong to the night or to the darkness. So then, let us not be like others, who are asleep, but let us be alert and self-controlled. For those who sleep, sleep at night, and those who get drunk, get drunk at night. But since we belong to the day, let us be self-controlled, putting on faith and love as a breastplate, and the hope of salvation as a helmet. For God did not appoint us to suffer wrath but to receive salvation through our Lord Jesus Christ. He died for us so that, whether we are awake or asleep, we may live together with him. Therefore encourage one another and build each other up, just as in fact you are doing.

KEY VERSE
for Lessons 5–9

"So in everything, do to others what you would have them do to you."

(Matthew 7:12a)

People used to call it edification. Now we call it encouragement or building others up. Whatever we call it, it's something the Bible encourages us to do. And it's the opposite of putting people down.

Put-downs are a way of life for today's fifth- and sixth-graders. They receive them and often hurl them right back. But even with snappy comebacks, put-downs still do their damage. And kids today seem to have more trouble with positive self-esteem than ever before.

Use this lesson to help kids see how damaging put-downs are and how helpful building up is.

GETTING THE POINT

Students will
- ◆ examine feelings related to put-downs,
- ◆ experience behavior in the dark and in the light,
- ◆ be tempted to retaliate when attacked, and
- ◆ build up others in the class.

THIS LESSON AT A GLANCE

Before the lesson, collect the necessary items from the Learning Lab for the activities you plan to use. Refer to the pictures in the margin to see what each item looks like.

SECTION	MINUTES	WHAT STUDENTS WILL DO	LEARNING LAB SUPPLIES	CLASSROOM SUPPLIES
ATTENTION GRABBER	up to 8	**The Power of Encouragement**—Try to get an eagle higher off the ground than anyone else can and compare the experience to building others up.	Balancing eagle	
BIBLE EXPLORATION AND APPLICATION	up to 12	**Caught in the Light**—Experience being mischievous in the dark and stopping when a light comes on and then explore 1 Thessalonians 5:4-8.	Inflatable eyeball, fiber optic flashlight	Bibles
	up to 15	**Battle of the Put-Downs**—Have a wadded-newspaper battle and explore 1 Thessalonians 5:8.		Bibles, newspapers, magazines, masking tape
	up to 10	**Want a Lift?**—Read 1 Thessalonians 5:10-11 and then lift each other up in the air and tell great qualities they see in each other.		Bibles
CLOSING	up to 10	**Encouragement Pact**—Write down the encouraging things others say about them and then commit to building up each other always.		Paper, pens, tape
MODULE REVIEW	up to 5	**Reflection**—Review what they've learned during the past five lessons.		

Remember to make photocopies of the "Table Talk" handout (p. 97) to send home with your kids. "Table Talk" is a valuable tool for helping fifth- and sixth-graders talk with their parents about what they're learning in class.

THE LESSON

When kids arrive, remind them that you'll sound the *noisemaker* when you need their attention and you'll wait for all of them to look at you without talking before you continue.

Before you begin the lesson, ask kids about last week's "Table Talk" discussions. Use questions such as "How were you able to pray for a hurting person?" and "How did you see God's help for your family?" However, be careful not to alienate students whose families chose not to use "Table Talk."

ATTENTION GRABBER

THE POWER OF ENCOURAGEMENT

(up to 8 minutes)

LEARNING LAB

If possible, do this activity outside or in a room with a very high ceiling. Form teams of six or fewer. Hold up the *balancing eagle* and say: **We're going to hold a little contest to see how high off the ground your group can get this eagle—without letting it fall. For now, look around the room and talk with your teammates about ideas for how you can lift this eagle safely up as high as possible without letting it fall.**

After a few minutes, have teams take turns using their ideas to lift the *balancing eagle* as high off the ground as possible—without letting it fall. Congratulate each group's efforts. When all the groups have made the attempt, have them discuss these questions:

◆ **What makes you feel like an eagle soaring on the heights?**

◆ **How was trying to lift the eagle up high like trying to build other people up in real life?**

◆ **How can people help you feel encouraged about yourself and your life?**

◆ **Is it important to you to feel encouraged by other people? Why or why not?**

◆ **Why is it important for you to encourage others?**

Say: **We all want to soar like eagles in life. But, more often than not, we can't fly very high without the support and encouragement of others.** ☞ **God wants us to build people up. And we're going to begin today.**

TEACHER TIP

It's important to say The Point just as it's written in each activity. Repeating The Point over and over will help kids remember it and apply it to their lives.

☞ THE **POINT**

LEARNING LAB

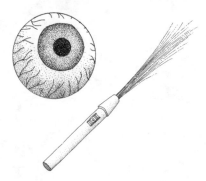

BIBLE INSIGHT

Paul uses symbolic language, quite common in biblical and non-biblical writings of the period, to contrast the Christians' lives with the unbelievers'. First, Paul encourages Christians not to live wicked lives as "sons of darkness" do, but rather to live as "sons of light." He further explains the actions of those who live in darkness as typical nighttime activities of sleeping and getting drunk. Second, Paul compares living in spiritual "daylight" in verse 8 as being like an alert soldier on duty. The armor associated with a soldier protects a Christian from the evil of those living in the darkness.

THE **POINT** ☞

BIBLE EXPLORATION
AND APPLICATION

CAUGHT IN THE LIGHT

(up to 12 minutes)

Take kids to a totally dark room, and encourage them to make funny faces at each other in the dark. Warn kids to watch out for the "Seeing Eye" that will appear from time to time. Anyone making a funny face at another person when the eye appears must go sit in the corner for the rest of the game.

When kids understand the rules, start the activity. When the kids have become pretty wild, point the *fiber optic flashlight* directly into the *inflatable eyeball* and turn on the flashlight. Ask kids to identify anyone who was making funny faces at them when the light came on, and instruct those kids to go sit in the corner. Then turn off the *fiber optic flashlight,* and encourage kids to continue. Shine the flashlight into the *inflatable eyeball* one or two more times. Then stop the game and return to your meeting room.

You probably will notice a difference in the way kids act after the light came on the first time. If you don't, ask kids why they didn't change their behavior, since they knew what would happen if they didn't behave. Discuss how it's easier to get away with wrong things in the dark than in the light. Ask:

◆ **What were you thinking when the lights were off?**

◆ **Did your behavior change when the "Seeing Eye" appeared? Why or why not?**

Say: **The Bible uses images of light and dark to explain how we should live. Here's what I mean.** Have a volunteer read aloud **1 Thessalonians 5:4-8** while the other kids follow along.

Have kids find partners and discuss the following questions together. Kids will want to keep their own Bibles handy and opened to **1 Thessalonians 5:4-8.**

After asking each question, allow time for volunteers to share their answers with the whole class. Ask:

◆ **How is our experience in the dark and the light similar to what's described in this passage?**

◆ **What do you think it means to belong to the light and to the day?**

Say: **People sometimes put others down to build themselves up. But** ☞ **God wants us to build people up. We can live in the light all the time, knowing that God always sees us and is happy when we're helping other**

people instead of hurting them. Unfortunately, we often hurt people instead of helping them. Let's see what that feels like.

BATTLE OF THE PUT-DOWNS

(up to 15 minutes)

Form two teams. Give one team a stack of newspapers. Give the other team a stack of magazines. Use a long piece of masking tape to divide the room into two sides. Have the team with the magazines stand a few feet back from the line. This should keep kids from being hurt because the newspaper wads will lose much of their force.

Say: **We're going to have a battle. The team with newspapers is to wad the pages up and use them to attack the team on the other side of the line without crossing the line. Anyone hit in the head with a wad of newspaper must sit down. The team members with the magazines can use the magazines as shields to protect their faces and heads.**

The kids with the magazines will probably begin picking up newspaper wads thrown at them and throw them back. After two or three minutes, stop the action. Ask:

◆ **Magazine Team, what was it like to be attacked?**

◆ **Did the magazines protect you? Why or why not?**

◆ **Why did you start throwing newspaper wads back?**

◆ **How was this battle like the way people "throw" put-downs in real life?**

Say: **Let's take a look at a passage that talks about protecting ourselves.** Have a volunteer read aloud **1 Thessalonians 5:8-9** while the others follow along.

Have kids quickly turn to partners and take turns answering the following question. Then have volunteers share the answers their partners gave with the whole class. Ask:

◆ **How do faith and love protect us?**

Say: **With God on our side, we don't have to fight back. When people cut us down, we can take it because we know we're important to God.** Ask:

◆ **How does knowing God gives you salvation help you endure put-downs and persecution today?**

Say: ☞ **God wants us to build people up. When we do, we will please God. We're going to practice building each other up right now.**

TEACHER TIP

Encourage active participation in the discussion by following up kids' answers with questions such as "What did you mean by that?" and "Can you tell me more?"

KEY VERSE CONNECTION

"So in everything, do to others what you would have them do to you" (Matthew 7:12a).

Fifth- and sixth-grade classrooms are prime breeding spots for cliques. And with cliques usually come put-downs, exclusions, and hurt feelings that can last a lifetime. Voice the Key Verse often to remind kids that no one likes a put-down.

 THE **POINT**

WANT A LIFE?

(up to 10 minutes)

THE POINT

Read aloud **1 Thessalonians 5:10-11.** Then say: 📖 **God wants us to build people up, and we're going to start doing that right now.**

Have kids form teams of six. Have members of each team seat one of the team members in a chair and then surround him or her and grip the chair with both hands. On the count of three, have members of each team carefully and slowly lift the seated team member up to their shoulders, being careful to keep the chair level at all times. Once the seated person is lifted high, have team members take turns calling out great qualities they think that person has. For example, kids may say "funny," "kind," or "smart."

After kids have called out several great qualities, have them carefully lower the seated person and give someone else a turn. Have teams continue until everyone has had a chance to sit in the chair.

When teams have finished, have them sit on the floor in a circle and wait for the other teams to finish. Then ask:

- ◆ **What was it like to be lifted in the air?**
- ◆ **How did the compliments make you feel? Why?**
- ◆ **What are other ways you can build each other up?**

Say: **It feels great to be built up by others and to build up others. Let's commit to doing that now.**

> ## TEACHER TIP
>
> For safety, don't use a folding chair for this activity. If mishandled, a folding chair could begin to close, possibly pinching fingers of those holding the chair.

TABLE TALK

Christian education extends beyond the classroom into the home. Photocopy the "Table Talk" handout (p. 97) for this week, and send it home with your kids. Encourage kids and parents to use the handout to spark meaningful discussion on this week's topic. Follow up next week by asking kids how their discussions with their families went.

CLOSING

ENCOURAGEMENT PACT

(up to 10 minutes)

Give each person paper and a pen, and have them write down the great things they heard others say about them in the previous activity. (If you didn't do the previous activity, have kids form foursomes and have group members each share one or two great qualities they see in each of their group members.)

Have kids write their names on their papers. Then provide tape so kids can tape their papers to one of your meeting-room walls. When everyone is finished, have kids form a semicircle around their papers and encourage kids to read what they said about each other. Say: **God wants us to build people up, and it's not hard to see why. The encouraging words on your papers are powerful. We can always help each other remember just how special we are. If you're willing, let's make a pact with each other before God that we will always strive to see the best in one another and remind each other of how special we really are.**

Encourage kids to pray, committing before God to always try to see the best in others and to encourage them instead of putting them down.

☞ THE POINT

MODULE REVIEW

REFLECTION

(up to 5 minutes)

Say: **Today we've learned that ☞ God wants us to build people up. But during the past five class sessions, we've learned a lot about relationships. Let's take a moment now to think about what we've gained from those class sessions.**

Form a circle. Go around the circle and have students take turns completing the following sentences (rotate the sentence completions until each person has completed one):

◆ One constructive way to solve conflicts is... *To pray) show kindnes-respect*
◆ It's important to forgive others because... *he forgave us*

☞ THE POINT

◆ We can develop solid friendships with the opposite sex by... *Learning to cooperate- communicate*

◆ Standing up against pressure may be tough, but it's important because... *God will honor us for Standing Strong*

◆ One thing I can do to build others up is... *to give complinents*

When you've gone around the circle, thank students for participating in this series on relationships.

To dismiss, have kids go around the room and tell each other reasons they're glad they've experienced these lessons together.

Discussion Starters

◆ What are simple ways to tear others down? to build them up?

◆ Tell about a time an "insignificant" event either brightened or darkened your day.

Family Building

*For Kids Only: Try to give five compliments to others every day this week.

*For Parents Only: Take some time to deliberately affirm each of your kids. Consider making a certificate for each child commemorating something about who he or she is. For example, you could make a certificate that celebrates your son's or daughter's honesty as shown in the way he or she returned a found item.

*For the Family: Think of the grumpiest and cruelest person you know. As a family, think of one simple way to build that person up. Try to come up with an idea that the person can accept. Don't let fear of a negative response prevent you from reaching out.

Something to Think About

A man walked from San Francisco to New York. After the journey, a friend asked the traveler which part was most difficult. He expected the walker to say something about the mountain ranges he crossed, the deserts endured, or the weather he encountered. But instead the walker replied, "What almost defeated me in my journey across the continent was the sand in my shoes."

(from *Knight's Master Book of 4,000 Illustrations* by Walter B. Knight)

The little things in life can make all the difference. Think about the last time you were in a bad mood. What put you there? It certainly could have come from a major disaster in your life. But your bad mood was most likely influenced by a small disappointment, a strange look from a close friend, or another relatively insignificant event.

Encouragement is an incredible thing. It's really not to hard to do, and it makes an incredible difference. Try it for a day. Smile at the people you meet; give each person a small compliment; offer a quick word of thanks to a friend. Pay special attention to how each little act affects those around you. Then at the end of the day, take note of how doing small, kind things for others affected your day.

"Each of us should please his neighbor for his good, to build him up" **(Romans 15:2).**

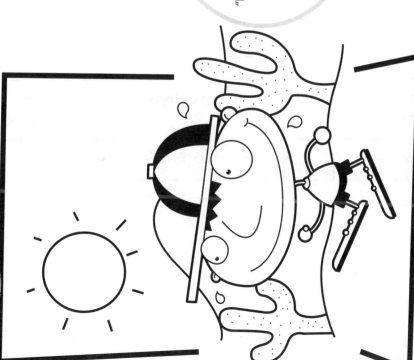

Table Talk

Group's **hands·On BiBLE** curriculum™

MONEY AND TIME

We're in a society where many kids have more discretionary annual income than many Third World families have total annual income. And they have more free time than kids of any other generation. Today kids struggle with whether to spend their money at the movies or to buy the latest CD. They wonder if they should spend their afternoons at the mall or the recreation center.

How kids spend their money and their time may not seem to be much of an issue to the culture at large. But it's an issue to God. Stewardship—the use of one's resources in accountability to someone else—may be a new topic to your fifth- and sixth-graders. They need to learn, though, that how they use their resources affects others and that God holds them accountable for what they do with what they have.

These four lessons will help kids uncover why stewardship is important, and they'll teach kids skills for using their money and time in ways that please God.

FOUR LESSONS ON MONEY AND TIME

LESSON	PAGE	THE POINT	THE BIBLE BASIS
10—Too Many Things	100	If we focus our lives on Jesus, possessions become less important.	Mark 10:17-31
11—Using Money Wisely	110	God wants us to use our resources wisely.	Matthew 25:14-29
12—Making the Most of Opportunities	119	We can serve God by doing good things for others.	Galatians 6:7-10
13—Time for God	129	God wants us to set aside time to spend with him.	Daniel 6:6-10

THE SIGNAL

During the lessons on money and time, your signal to get kids back together during activities will be to sound the *noisemaker* found in the Learning Lab. In response to sounding the *noisemaker,* have kids stop what they're doing and focus on you for their next instructions.

Tell kids about this signal before the lesson begins. Explain that it's important to respond to this signal quickly so the class can do as many fun activities as possible.

THE TIME STUFFER

LEARNING LAB

The Time Stuffer for the four lessons on money and time is a poster called "My Future," which is found in the Learning Lab. Display the poster in a prominent place in your meeting area, and put paper and pencils nearby. The directions on the poster instruct kids to answer the questions about their future.

Use the Time Stuffer to constructively occupy kids' time before your class starts, when some kids finish an activity earlier than others, or just when you have extra time with a few kids.

By the end of the month you'll have an interesting display, plus kids will have fun seeing how others filled in the blanks.

REMEMBERING THE BIBLE

Each four- or five-week module focuses on a Key Bible Verse. The Key Verse for this module is "But seek first his kingdom and his righteousness, and all these things will be given to you as well" **(Matthew 6:33).**

Look for the Key Verse Connection in the margin of each lesson to tie the Key Verse to that week's Point.

LESSON 10

TOO MANY THINGS

THE POINT

☞ **If we focus our lives on Jesus, possessions become less important.**

THE BIBLE BASIS

Mark 10:17-31

As Jesus started on his way, a man ran up to him and fell on his knees before him. "Good teacher," he asked, "what must I do to inherit eternal life?"

"Why do you call me good?" Jesus answered. "No one is good—except God alone. You know the commandments: 'Do not murder, do not commit adultery, do not steal, do not give false testimony, do not defraud, honor your father and mother.' "

"Teacher," he declared, "all these I have kept since I was a boy."

Jesus looked at him and loved him. "One thing you lack," he said. "Go, sell everything you have and give to the poor, and you will have treasure in heaven. Then come, follow me."

At this the man's face fell. He went away sad, because he had great wealth.

Jesus looked around and said to his disciples, "How hard it is for the rich to enter the kingdom of God!"

The disciples were amazed at his words. But Jesus said again, "Children, how hard it is to enter the kingdom of God! It is easier for a camel to go through the eye of a needle than for a rich man to enter the kingdom of God."

The disciples were even more amazed, and said to each other, "Who then can be saved?"

Jesus looked at them and said, "With man this is impossible, but not with God; all things are possible with God."

Peter said to him, "We have left everything to follow you!"

"I tell you the truth," Jesus replied, "no one who has left home or brothers or sisters or mother or father or children or fields for me and the gospel will fail to receive a hundred times as much in this present age (homes, brothers, sisters, mothers, children and fields—and with them, persecutions) and in the age to come, eternal life. But many who are first will be last, and the last first."

KEY *VERSE*

for Lessons 10–13

"But seek first his kingdom and his righteousness, and all these things will be given to you as well."

(Matthew 6:33)

Throughout the Bible, God warns that money can be a problem for people. People often think of wealth as a goal rather than as a resource. God never says that money is evil; money is merely a tool that can be used wisely or foolishly. But using wealth to buy things that better our standing in the world can jeopardize our relationships with God.

It's difficult to teach kids in a consumer-conscious culture that it's possible to have too many possessions. Kids are targets for the latest fashions, games, and entertainment activities. But it's important for them to learn that what they'll get from a relationship with God is far more valuable than the things they possess or the fun things they do.

Other Scriptures used in this lesson are **Matthew 6:25-34** and **Colossians 3:1-3.**

GETTING THE POINT

Students will
- talk about how things might get in the way of their relationships with Jesus,
- experience their real need for possessions and money,
- discover what the Bible says about things that are really worth life investments, and
- determine how they can best keep a proper focus in life.

THIS LESSON AT A GLANCE

Before the lesson, collect the necessary items from the Learning Lab for the activities you plan to use. Refer to the pictures in the margin to see what each item looks like.

SECTION	MINUTES	WHAT STUDENTS WILL DO	LEARNING LAB SUPPLIES	CLASSROOM SUPPLIES
ATTENTION GRABBER	up to 10	**Ring Grab**—Compete to collect rings that represent possessions.	Plastic rings, bottle rings, neon shoelaces	
BIBLE EXPLORATION AND APPLICATION	up to 15	**Stay Afloat**—Build boats for floating rocks, compare the experience to how possessions can't keep us afloat, and read Matthew 6:25-34.	Pumice rocks	Bible, screwdriver, hammer, bucket of water, paper
	up to 15	**Virtual Mint**—Look at a dollar bill through a prism scope and discuss attitudes about money while exploring Mark 10:17-31.	Prism scopes	Bibles, two one-dollar bills, "The Price" hand-outs (p. 108), pencils
	up to 10	**Picture My Life**—Draw pictures while being distracted before exploring Colossians 3:1-3.	Whip whistle, noisemakers, handblasters, clacker balls, fiber optic flashlight, bottle rings	Bibles, markers, paper
CLOSING	up to 10	**Focus Check**—Determine how to keep a proper focus on the things that are truly important.	Cassette: "More Precious Than Silver," "Lyrics Poster"	"The Price" handouts from the "Virtual Mint" activity, cassette player

Remember to make photocopies of the "Table Talk" handout (p. 109) to send home with your kids. "Table Talk" is a valuable tool for helping fifth- and sixth-graders talk with their parents about what they're learning in class.

THE LESSON

As kids arrive, teach them the signal for the quarter. Tell kids that whenever you sound the *noisemaker,* they're to stop what they're doing and look at you without talking. Explain that when you have everyone's attention, you'll continue the lesson.

Before you begin the lesson, ask kids about last week's "Table Talk" discussions. Use questions such as "How were you able to compliment others?" and "What happened when you built another person up?" However, be careful not to alienate students whose families chose not to use "Table Talk."

ATTENTION GRABBER

RING GRAB

(up to 10 minutes)

Say: **These *plastic rings* and *bottle rings* I have represent all our possessions—all the "stuff"—that we collect over our lifetimes.**

Form four teams, and give each team one of the *neon shoelaces*. Have each team go to a different corner of the room. Throw all the *plastic rings* and *bottle rings* into the air. Do your best to scatter them all over the room. Explain to the kids that they can do anything short of hurting other people to gather as many rings as possible in thirty seconds. The teams must string the rings on their *neon shoelaces* as they gather them.

After thirty seconds, call time. Have teams count only the rings they've strung on their *neon shoelaces*.

Have kids sit with their team members to discuss the following questions.

Ask:

◆ **What went through your mind as you were trying to get your rings?**

◆ **How did you respond when I called time? Explain.**

◆ **How was gathering the rings like the way people collect possessions in real life? How was it different?**

◆ **Did you try to collect one of the larger *bottle rings* or lots of the smaller *plastic rings*? Explain.**

◆ **How do the different rings represent the different things we try to collect in real life?**

◆ **What are some of the reasons people try to get "stuff" in real life?**

◆ **How can possessions and money be bad things?**

Say: ***Things* aren't bad. We all collect "stuff." But when collecting possessions is all we care about, it's easy to lose our perspective and allow things to become more important than God.**  **If we focus our lives on Jesus, possessions become less important. Let's explore how to do this.**

Collect the Learning Lab items for future use.

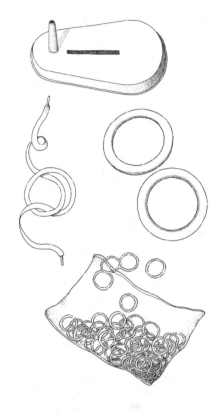

TEACHER TIP

It's important to say The Point just as it's written in each activity. Repeating The Point over and over throughout the lesson will help kids remember it and apply it to their lives.

✎ THE **POINT**

LEARNING LAB

TEACHER TIP

The *pumice rocks* break easily with the use of a screwdriver. Set a rock down on a hard surface and use a hammer to gently tap or push a screwdriver through the rock to break it in half.

━BIBLE *INSIGHT*

Matthew was a tax collector when he was called to follow Jesus. At that time, tax collectors were able to gain considerable wealth by collecting taxes in excess of what the Roman government required, a practice that was condoned by the Romans. That such a man, so focused on material matters, would be invited into the kingdom demonstrates the generosity of the reconciliation Christ offers.

TEACHER TIP

Some of the boats might sink immediately. If this happens, have all the kids take their boats out of the water. Skip the first section of debriefing questions and lead kids directly to **Matthew 6:25-34.** Then discuss the second set of questions that follows the reading of the Scripture.

THE **POINT** 🖝

BIBLE EXPLORATION AND APPLICATION

▐ STAY AFLOAT

(up to 15 minutes)

Before this activity, use a screwdriver and a hammer to break the *pumice rocks* so that there is one piece of *pumice rock* for every four kids in your group. Put a bucket of water in the middle of the room.

Have kids form groups of four. Say: **I'm going to give each group one "pet" rock that symbolizes life.**

Give each group a small *pumice rock* piece and a sheet of paper. Say: **The bucket of water stands for the troubles that come in life. With your group, use your piece of paper to construct a raft or boat that will keep your rock afloat in the water.**

Give groups about three minutes to construct their boats. Then say: **I'd like you to put your rock on your boat and put your boat in the water.** Give kids the opportunity to watch their boats for about a minute and then set a sheet of paper over the bucket. Ask:

◆ **How are the boats like money and possessions? How are they different?**

◆ **What things in your life keep you afloat when things get difficult or rough?**

◆ **Does your rock need the boat to stay afloat?**

◆ **Do you need money or possessions to keep going through difficult times? Explain.**

Have five volunteers read **Matthew 6:25-34** by each reading two verses aloud. Take the sheet of paper off of the top of the bucket, and say: **I'd like you to take your boat out from under your rock and watch what happens.**

After kids observe the floating *pumice rocks,* ask:

◆ **How does God keep us afloat in difficult times?**

◆ **What things can God do that money and possessions cannot?**

◆ **What place does God want money and possessions to take in our lives?**

Say: **Possessions and money appear to keep our lives going and they appear to keep us happy. However, the truth is that *God* takes care of our needs and *he* keeps us content and full of peace. We don't need to chase after money and possessions because God gives us everything we need. 🖝 As we focus our lives on Jesus, possessions**

become less important.

Set the *pumice rocks* aside to dry before returning them to the Learning Lab.

VIRTUAL MINT 📖

(up to 15 minutes)

Have kids form two groups, and have the groups go to different areas in the room. Give each group a *prism scope*. Set a crisp one-dollar bill on the floor near each group.

Say: **I want each of you to use a *prism scope* to look at a dollar bill. As you look at the dollar bill, make sure it's in the center of your view. After you've looked at the bill through the *prism scope,* come over to me for more instructions.**

As kids come to you, have them form groups of four and give each group a copy of "The Price" handout (p. 108) and a pencil. Encourage groups to discuss and answer the questions on the handout. When all the groups have finished, give each group an opportunity to share what it discussed with the entire class.

Say: **The man in the Bible story you read may have loved Jesus, but he obviously loved money more. Every possession and dollar we have is a gift from God. God gave us possessions to enjoy and use while we are on earth. But it's important that we *never* put God's gifts or blessings in front of God.**

📖 **If we focus on Jesus, we'll find that possessions are less important. No amount of money is worth sacrificing our relationship with Jesus. Our relationship with Jesus lasts forever. Money and possessions—no matter how much or how wonderful they are—only last while we are on this earth.**

Collect the *prism scopes* for future use.

PICTURE MY LIFE 📖

(up to 10 minutes)

Choose one volunteer for every three to four students. Take the volunteers into a corner of the room and tell them secretly that when you say "go," they're to act as distracters to the rest of the class. Give each volunteer one or two of the following gizmos: the *whip whistle,* the *noisemakers,* the *handblasters,* the *clacker balls,* the *fiber optic flashlight,* and the *bottle rings.*

KEY VERSE CONNECTION

"But seek first his kingdom and his righteousness, and all these things will be given to you as well" (Matthew 6:33).

Kids may have trouble differentiating between what they need and what they want, especially in today's material world. Expensive sports shoes, designer labels, and the newest computer game may seem like necessities. Use this Key Verse to show kids that if they seek God first, all their real needs will be met.

 THE **POINT**

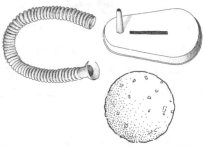

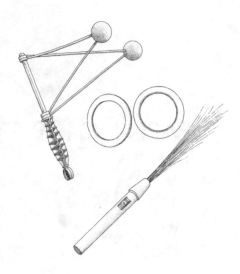

Tell your volunteers to use the gizmos to keep others from completing the project you're about to assign. For example, the student with the *bottle rings* could toss them onto the papers that others draw on. Encourage kids to be obnoxious but to avoid hurting anyone in any way.

Distribute markers and paper to everyone in the class, including the distracters. Say: **You'll have three minutes to draw pictures that tell us four things about you: (1) what you like to do, (2) what you'd like to have, (3) what you'd like to be, and (4) ways you can include Jesus in your life. When time is up, you'll each take a turn telling the rest of the class about your pictures. Ready? Go!**

Call time after three minutes, and collect the Learning Lab items for future use. Ask for a show of hands of those who finished. Then form pairs, and have partners take turns answering the following questions.

Ask:

◆ **How did you feel when you were interrupted?**

◆ **How did these distractions keep you from concentrating on your task?**

◆ **How is this like the way our possessions can distract us from what's important?**

◆ **What things in your life are currently distracting you from your relationship with God?**

Have volunteers share what they talked about with their partners. Then ask for a volunteer to read **Colossians 3:1-3** aloud while the others follow along.

Say: **Our possessions can be distractions that keep us from focusing on our relationship with God. But ☞ if we focus our lives on Jesus, our possessions become less important to us and Jesus becomes more important.**

THE **POINT** ☞

TABLE TALK

Christian education extends beyond the classroom into the home. Photocopy the "Table Talk" handout (p. 109) for this week, and send it home with your kids. Encourage kids and parents to use the handout to spark meaningful discussion on this week's topic. Follow up next week by asking kids how their discussions with their families went.

CLOSING

FOCUS CHECK

(up to 10 minutes)

Have kids return to their groups from the "Virtual Mint" activity. Say: **I'd like you to take another look at the last three questions on "The Price" handouts.**  **If we focus on Jesus, our possessions are less important. So as a group, I'd like you to think about what you can do to help you focus on Jesus.**

Give groups about two minutes to brainstorm. Then direct students to think about the three most important things in their own lives. Have kids take a minute alone to pray and think about how they can keep their focus on their relationship with Jesus and on what's important.

Say: **One way to keep our focus on Jesus is to worship him. We're going to close our time doing just that by singing "More Precious Than Silver."** Lead kids in singing "More Precious Than Silver" from the *cassette tape*. The lyrics are printed on a poster found in the Learning Lab. Ask:

◆ **How is Jesus more precious to you than any of your possessions?**

Have kids answer this question in a brief silent prayer to close.

Return the *cassette tape* and the "Lyrics Poster" to the Learning Lab for future use.

LEARNING LAB

TEACHER TIP

If you didn't do the "Virtual Mint" activity, write the last three questions from "The Price" handout (p. 108) on a sheet of newsprint. Have kids form groups of four and discuss the questions before they begin the "Focus Check" activity.

The Price

Discuss each of the following questions with your group. Then write down one answer for each question.

◆ Imagine that all the dollar bills you saw as you looked through the *prism scope* were real, what would you be willing to trade for the money?

◆ Imagine that all the bills you saw were $100 bills. Would you be willing to tell a lie for that much money? Would you be willing to disobey your parents? Why or why not?

◆ How much money would someone have to give you to get you to quit going to church? to stop being a Christian?

◆ Read Mark 10:17-31. How much money do you think this man had?

◆ Why do you think he wasn't able to give up his money?

◆ Would you have made the same choice? Why or why not?

◆ What is the most important thing in life?

◆ What are the next three most important things in life?

◆ What are these things worth?

Table Talk

Group's Hands-On BIBLE Curriculum

Discussion Starters

- What possession do you want more than anything else?
- Why do you want it?
- Do you think you'll be satisfied when you get that possession? Explain.

Family Building

*For Kids Only: Give away one possession to a people-helping organization (such as a safe house for young boys or girls). Try to give something that is valuable to you instead of something that you don't want or use.

*For Parents Only: Help your family understand the needs of others by serving at an organization designed to help meet the needs of the hurting, lonely, or poor.

*For the Family: Start a family charity jar. Cut a slit in the top of a jar lid and glue cide to the jar. When the jar is full, decide as a family who the money will go to and carefully break the jar open and take the money to those in need.

Something to Think About

Picture a stack of one million one-dollar bills piled on top of each other (over six hundred feet tall!). Now imagine that there are 36,400 of those stacks next to each other (enough to fill a high school basketball court!). According to the July 14, 1997 issue of The Salt Lake Tribune, that's how much money ($36.4 billion) Bill Gates had in 1997. The Walton family (heirs to the Wal-Mart fortune) had 27.6 billion dollars. Written out, that number looks like this: $27,600,000,000.

It's easy to get disgusted or jealous of the riches people like these possess. It's easy to think that they can't possibly need the money and that we could put it to much better use.

Before you start to get angry, jealous, and frustrated, think about those who could say the same thing about you. Think of the families who don't know if they'll see tomorrow because they haven't had any food. Think of your neighbors or the people across town who have less than you do. How have you used your riches to help them? You don't need a million dollars to make a difference. You can make a difference with one dollar or even by giving a half hour of your time.

"No one can serve two masters. Either he will hate the one and love the other, or he will be devoted to the one and despise the other. You cannot serve both God and Money"

(Matthew 6:24).

Too Many Things, Week 10

LESSON 11

USING MONEY WISELY

THE POINT

☞ **God wants us to use our resources wisely.**

THE BIBLE BASIS

Matthew 25:14-29

"Again, it will be like a man going on a journey, who called his servants and entrusted his property to them. To one he gave five talents of money, to another two talents, and to another one talent, each according to his ability. Then he went on his journey. The man who had received the five talents went at once and put his money to work and gained five more. So also, the one with the two talents gained two more. But the man who had received the one talent went off, dug a hole in the ground and hid his master's money.

"After a long time the master of those servants returned and settled accounts with them. The man who had received the five talents brought the other five. 'Master,' he said, 'you entrusted me with five talents. See, I have gained five more.'

"His master replied, 'Well done, good and faithful servant! You have been faithful with a few things; I will put you in charge of many things. Come and share your master's happiness!'

"The man with the two talents also came. 'Master,' he said, 'you entrusted me with two talents; see, I have gained two more.'

"His master replied, 'Well done, good and faithful servant! You have been faithful with a few things; I will put you in charge of many things. Come and share your master's happiness!'

"Then the man who had received the one talent came. 'Master,' he said, 'I knew that you are a hard man, harvesting where you have not sown and gathering where you have not scattered seed. So I was afraid and went out and hid your talent in the ground. See, here is what belongs to you.'

"His master replied, 'You wicked, lazy servant! So you knew that I harvest where I have not sown and gather where I have not scattered seed? Well then, you should have put my money on deposit with the bankers, so that when I returned I would have received it back with interest.

KEY *VERSE*
for Lessons 10–13

"But seek first his kingdom and his righteousness, and all these things will be given to you as well."

(Matthew 6:33)

" 'Take the talent from him and give it to the one who has the ten talents. For everyone who has will be given more, and he will have an abundance. Whoever does not have, even what he has will be taken from him.' "

This parable uses an example that would have been familiar to Jesus' listeners. Servants were often trusted to manage their master's property. Jesus told his audience that it was no different with God. Everything we have is a resource that God has entrusted to us. And we're accountable to God for how we use these resources.

But that's not the message kids hear most often. The world teaches that what we have belongs solely to us and that no one can tell us how to spend our own money.

Use this lesson to teach kids that all things belong to God, though he trusts them to us. We're to be responsible stewards of God's wealth, using it wisely to increase his kingdom.

Other Scriptures used in this lesson are **1 Timothy 6:18-19** and **1 John 2:15-17.**

GETTING THE POINT

Students will
- ◆ talk about their priorities for using money,
- ◆ discover what the Bible says about being stewards of the resources God gives them, and
- ◆ think about how they might use their resources to please God.

THIS LESSON AT A GLANCE

Before the lesson, collect the necessary items from the Learning Lab for the activities you plan to use. Refer to the pictures in the margin to see what each item looks like.

SECTION	MINUTES	WHAT STUDENTS WILL DO	LEARNING LAB SUPPLIES	CLASSROOM SUPPLIES
ATTENTION GRABBER	up to 10	**Wacky Whistles**—Think of new uses for the whip whistle.	Whip whistle	
BIBLE EXPLORATION AND APPLICATION	up to 14	**Stewardsville 1**—Decide how to spend money in a fictitious town and then explore Matthew 25:14-29.	Plastic rings	Bibles, chalkboard and chalk or newsprint and marker, tape
	up to 14	**Stewardsville 2**—Read 1 John 2:15-17 and then go back to town and decide how to spend money, including God in the decisions.	Plastic rings	Bibles, chalkboard and chalk or newsprint and marker
	up to 12	**Hidden Treasures**—Discover special resources they have and examine 1 Timothy 6:18-19.	All Learning Lab items	Bibles, tape
CLOSING	up to 10	**Turn Over a New Leaf**—Examine the ways they've wasted the resources God has given them and commit to using God's resources more wisely.	Cassette: "More Precious Than Silver," "Lyrics Poster"	Paper, pencils, cassette player

Remember to make photocopies of the "Table Talk" handout (p. 118) to send home with your kids. "Table Talk" is a valuable tool for helping fifth- and sixth-graders talk with their parents about what they're learning in class.

THE LESSON

When kids arrive, remind them that you'll sound the *noisemaker* when you need their attention and you'll wait for all of them to look at you without talking before you continue.

Before you begin the lesson, ask kids about last week's "Table Talk" discussions. Use questions such as "What was it like to give away a valuable possession?" and "How are you doing with your charity jar?" However, be careful not to alienate students whose families chose not to use "Table Talk."

ATTENTION GRABBER

WACKY WHISTLES

(up to 10 minutes)

Have kids sit in a circle.

Say: **I'm going to pass around this *whip whistle*. Each of you will need to suggest one other possible use for it. No answer, regardless of how crazy it is, is too crazy. The only rule is that you may not repeat an answer.**

Pass the *whip whistle* from the Learning Lab around and get students' ideas. Ideas could include a snorkeling tube, a belt, or a telephone. If appropriate, have kids demonstrate their new ideas for using the *whip whistle*.

When the *whip whistle* comes back to you, ask:

◆ **How did you feel when it was your turn to say your idea? Explain.**

◆ **After a while, was it hard to think of new things to do with the *whip whistle*? Why or why not?**

Say: **Sometimes it's hard to think of new ideas for things we're used to using only one way. God gives us all kinds of resources, and the challenge for us is to come up with creative uses for them.**  **God wants us to use our resources wisely. Let's see how.**

Collect the *whip whistle* for future use.

LEARNING LAB

TEACHER TIP

It's important to say The Point just as it's written in each activity. Repeating The Point over and over throughout the lesson will help kids remember it and apply it to their lives.

🖎 THE **POINT**

BIBLE EXPLORATION AND APPLICATION

STEWARDSVILLE 1

(up to 14 minutes)

Have students form family groups of four or five.

Say: **You've all just become citizens of a town called Stewardsville. I'll give each of the family groups some of these *plastic rings*. They'll be your family group's money. You'll need to decide how to spend your money. This is all the money you'll get for a week, so your family group has to decide where to spend it and what portion of it goes to each place. First, we need to make a list of the possible places you can spend your money.**

Have kids think of places in town where they might want

LEARNING LAB

THE POINT ✍

to spend money. Write the ideas on a chalkboard or on a sheet of newsprint. Let kids come up with the ideas. They'll learn more if all the ideas are their own.

Tell kids that they don't need to decide how much things cost or what each ring is worth but rather, what proportion of their money they want to spend in each place. For example, they may want to spend half of their money at the pizza parlor, one-fourth of their money at the movie theater, and one-fourth of their money on new clothes. This exercise should reflect their spending priorities, not the cost of items.

Then turn the groups loose to make their decisions. Have them divide their rings into piles according to where they will spend them. Give kids three to five minutes to make their choices. Groups will need their ring piles for the next activity.

Next, have kids take turns answering the following questions for the whole group to hear. Ask:

◆ **What did you decide to spend the most money on?**
◆ **Where did you spend the least?**
◆ **How did you decide where to spend your money?**

Have each family group look up **Matthew 25:14-29,** and have group members take turns reading the verses aloud while the others follow along.

Say: **God has given us money and other resources to take care of just like the man in this story gave his servants money to take care of. We can use the money wisely like the first two servants did, or we can be foolish with what we've been given. The choice is ours.**

Then have kids take turns answering these questions in their family groups.

Ask:

◆ **What do you think our rewards will be for wisely using what God gives us?**
◆ **What do you think will happen if we aren't wise in the ways we use what God gives us?**
◆ **What does it mean to wisely use God's resources?**
◆ **What has God given you as a resource?**

Have volunteers share with the class what their groups said.

Say: ✍ **God wants us to use our resources wisely. But that takes practice. It's not always easy to decide the wisest way to use the things God gives us.**

STEWARDSVILLE 2

(up to 14 minutes)

Have the kids stay in their family groups. Have a volunteer read **1 John 2:15-17** as the other students follow along.

Then ask:

◆ **Does this passage mean that if we love God, we can't like any of our things? Explain.**

Say: **Now that we've looked at God's perspective on handling money, let's try our Stewardsville experiment again.**

Have the kids think of more places in town where they might want to spend money. Write them on a chalkboard or on a sheet of newsprint. Let the kids come up with all the ideas.

Say: **Decide if you want to make any changes about where your family will spend its money and about how much you'll spend. You don't have to spend at every place listed. This time, try to make your decisions based on what you think God would have your family group do from what we've seen in the Bible so far.**

Give the family groups only about three minutes to decide this time and, if necessary, rearrange their ring piles. Signal to bring kids back together. Then have family groups share their decisions with the rest of the class. Collect the *plastic rings* from each family. Put them back in the plastic bag and tape it shut. You'll use the bag of rings during the last Bible Exploration and Application activity.

Have kids form pairs, and have partners take turns answering the following questions.

Ask:

◆ **Does God want you to spend all your money on things like missions and the church? Why or why not?**

◆ **How do you decide how much money to spend on yourself and how much to give away?**

◆ **Is it wrong to spend money on fun things like going out for pizza or a movie? Why or why not?**

After volunteers share their partners' answers, say: **Including God in the picture when we think about using resources changes the way we make our decisions. God wants us to use our resources wisely. But he knows we need to use some of the money for ourselves. Using God's resources means thinking of God first and finding balance in how we spend our money. Let's find out what that means.**

━BIBLE *INSIGHT*

There's some debate among Christians about the place tithing (giving ten percent of one's income to the church) has in Christian stewardship. Christians who believe tithing is an important part of giving often point to Genesis 14:17-20 (Abraham gives ten percent of his possessions to Melchizedek); Leviticus 27:30 (God commands that a tithe belongs to him); and Deuteronomy 14:22-28 (the Israelites are commanded to set aside one-tenth of their crops).

Other Christians believe that since no New Testament verse clearly shows that we are to give ten percent of our income, each Christian should "give what he has decided in his heart to give, not reluctantly or under compulsion" (2 Corinthians 9:7b).

✎ THE **POINT**

LEARNING LAB

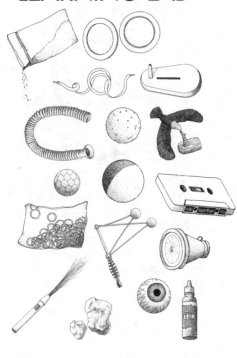

THE **POINT**

TEACHER TIP

Encourage active participation as students report back by following up kids' answers with questions such as "What did you mean by that?" and "Can you tell me more?"

HIDDEN TREASURES

(up to 12 minutes)

Say: **God gives each of us special gifts and possessions that we can use to serve him. Everything we have needs to be used wisely.**

Have the kids find some things in the room that represent gifts or possessions they have that can be wisely used as resources from God. Let the kids have access to everything in the Learning Lab. A student might choose an item such as the *sticky sports ball* to demonstrate how we should be careful not to throw our resources away.

Give the kids about three minutes to find items. Then have them each tell three other people in the class about the resources they have. Ask for volunteers to tell the entire class what resources they possess other than money.

Then gather kids in a circle. If you didn't do it earlier, put all the small *plastic rings* in the plastic bag and tape it so the rings can't fall out.

Have a volunteer read **1 Timothy 6:18-19** aloud while the others follow along.

Say: **God has made each of us rich. We may not have a lot of money, but we have many abilities and skills. Our resources include our talents, our possessions, and our time. This bag of rings represents all the resources that God gives us.**  **God wants us to use our resources wisely.**

Stand in the middle of the circle. Toss the bag of *plastic rings* to one student. As he or she catches the bag, mention one quality he or she has that is a resource to be used wisely. For example, you might say, "Janie, God has given you many resources. One of them is your ability to make others laugh. Use your special talent wisely."

Retrieve the bag and repeat the process with the other students, making sure you don't miss anyone. Return the bag of *plastic rings* to the Learning Lab.

TABLE TALK

Christian education extends beyond the classroom into the home. Photocopy the "Table Talk" handout (p. 118) for this week, and send it home with your kids. Encourage kids and parents to use the handout to spark meaningful discussion on this week's topic. Follow up next week by asking kids how their discussions with their families went.

CLOSING

TURN OVER A NEW LEAF

(up to 10 minutes)

Say: 📖 **God wants us to use our resources wisely. But remembering to be wise with our resources isn't always easy. We have so much that it's hard to be wise with all of it. But God can help us.**

Have kids find partners. Give each student a sheet of paper and a pencil. On one side have them write resources they don't always use wisely. Then have kids explain to their partners what they've written or drawn.

Have the kids turn their papers over and brainstorm with their partners as many ways as they can think of to wisely use those resources. Have partners each say a sentence prayer, asking God to help their partner be wise during the next week.

Say: **To help us remember to use our resources wisely, I'd like to close by singing "More Precious Than Silver." If this song comes to your mind during the week, think of how you're using the things God has given you. Think about whether you are using his gifts to bring glory to him.**

Lead kids in singing "More Precious Than Silver." Use the "Lyrics Poster" to assist you. Return the "Lyrics Poster" and the *cassette tape* for future use.

LEARNING LAB

Discussion Starters

- Do you spend your money wisely? Explain.
- Share an example of a time you wasted your money and a time you were a good steward of your money.
- How can you make it your pattern to spend your money wisely?

Family Building

*For Kids Only: Start an offering box. Put part of all the money you receive in the box. At the end of the month, give the money to your church.

*For Parents Only: If you don't have one, start a family budget. Begin by purchasing a budget planner at a local discount store.

*For the Family: Read the parable of the talents (Matthew 25:14-29). Give each person in your family five dollars. Challenge each family member to put the money to work and to make it grow. Think of ways to invest the money such as buying and trading baseball cards, using the money to repair an item and sell it, or putting an ad in the paper for furniture your family wants to sell. Commit to giving the proceeds to your church. After one month, see how much money your family made.

Something to Think About

Have you ever known someone who seemed to just throw away money? Take a look at a few things the United States government has done with your money:

- funded an $84,000 study to find out why people fall in love,
- spent $144,000 to see if pigeons follow human economic laws,
- spent $19 million to examine gas emissions from cow flatulence,
- funded an $800,000 restroom on Mt. McKinley,
- spent $219,000 to teach college students how to watch television,
- spent $2 million to construct an ancient Hawaiian canoe, and
- spent $57,000 to buy gold-embossed playing cards for Air Force Two.

(taken from *The Government Racket: Washington Waste From A to Z* by Martin L. Gross)

"For who makes you different from anyone else? What do you have that you did not receive? And if you did receive it, why do you boast as though you did not?"

(1 Corinthians 4:7).

We all make mistakes with the money God gives us. Sometimes we buy things we don't really need. Sometimes we spend money without finding the best deal. God doesn't want us to worry about money or to spend all our time thinking about the best way to spend it.

But God *does* want us to make good choices with how we use money. We need to remember that the money we have isn't really ours—it's God's. Whenever we get paid or get an allowance, we should ask God how he wants us to spend *his* money.

Table Talk

Group's hands-On BiBLE curriculum

Using Money Wisely, Week 11

Permission to photocopy this handout from Group's Hands-On Bible Curriculum™ for Grades 5 and 6 granted for local church use. Copyright © Group Publishing, Inc., P.O. Box 481, Loveland, CO 80539.

MAKING THE MOST OF OPPORTUNITIES

THE POINT

☞ **We can serve God by doing good things for others.**

THE BIBLE BASIS

Galatians 6:7-10

> Do not be deceived: God cannot be mocked. A man reaps what he sows. The one who sows to please his sinful nature, from that nature will reap destruction; the one who sows to please the Spirit, from the Spirit will reap eternal life. Let us not become weary in doing good, for at the proper time we will reap a harvest if we do not give up. Therefore, as we have opportunity, let us do good to all people, especially to those who belong to the family of believers.

KEY VERSE
for Lessons 10–13

"But seek first his kingdom and his righteousness, and all these things will be given to you as well."

(Matthew 6:33)

The early church needed a good press agent. People just didn't understand what Christianity was all about. Rumors circulating during the first century went so far as to label Christians as cannibals, an idea that came from misunderstanding what the Lord's Supper was. But Paul had more in mind than just what other people thought. He wanted to help the first-century Christians take advantage of opportunities God gave them every day to do good for others. Paul knew that acts of service glorify God and show the world a glimmer of what it's like to be loved by God. Service speaks to the world more powerfully than any press release could.

Christians can easily be numbed by all the problems they see around them. Fifth- and sixth-graders are no exception to this. But problems can be opportunities in disguise. By allowing God to help us see all the opportunities around us to serve others—and him—and then following through in action, we can obediently live as he commands.

Other Scriptures used in this lesson are **Ephesians 2:10** and **Luke 22:24-27.**

GETTING THE POINT

Students will
- ◆ experience how problems can become opportunities to serve others;
- ◆ examine what the Bible has to say about opportunities to serve God and others; and
- ◆ consider what skills, resources, and opportunities they have to offer God for service to others.

THIS LESSON AT A GLANCE

Before the lesson, collect the necessary items from the Learning Lab for the activities you plan to use. Refer to the pictures in the margin to see what each item looks like.

SECTION	MINUTES	WHAT STUDENTS WILL DO	LEARNING LAB SUPPLIES	CLASSROOM SUPPLIES
ATTENTION GRABBER	up to 10	**Risk It!**—Volunteers take a risk using handblasters.	Handblasters	
BIBLE EXPLORATION AND APPLICATION	up to 15	**Quest!**—Use Learning Lab items to smuggle Bibles to missionaries and discuss Ephesians 2:10.	Cassette: "Quest," all Learning Lab items	Bibles, cassette player, paper, pencils
	up to 10	**The Rub**—Handle pumice rocks as dust rubs off on their hands and discuss Galatians 6:7-10.	Pumice rocks	Bible
	up to 13	**I'll Be Your Server Today**—Learn to be prepared to meet others' needs and reflect on Jesus' words in Luke 22:24-27.	Handblasters	Bibles, photocopies of the "Cafe Service" handouts (p. 127), paper
CLOSING	up to 12	**Pass It On**—Affirm each other while spinning the clacker balls.	Clacker balls	

Remember to make photocopies of the "Table Talk" handout (p. 128) to send home with your kids. "Table Talk" is a valuable tool for helping fifth- and sixth-graders talk with their parents about what they're learning in class.

THE LESSON

When kids arrive, remind them that you'll sound the *noisemaker* when you need their attention and you'll wait for all of them to look at you without talking before you continue.

Before you begin the lesson, ask kids about last week's "Table Talk" discussions. Use questions such as "How are your contributions to your offering box going?" and "In what ways are you trying to raise money?" However, be careful not to alienate students whose families chose not to use "Table Talk."

ATTENTION GRABBER

RISK IT!

(up to 10 minutes)

Gather the kids in an open area of the room. Show them the *handblasters* found in the Learning Lab, and explain how they work. Then ask which kids have used them before. Warn those kids not to tell the rest of the class what it feels like to use them.

Ask for three to five volunteers who have never used *handblasters* before to try them. Let volunteers use them, but tell them not to say anything as they do. When all volunteers have used the *handblasters,* collect them for later use.

Ask the volunteers:

◆ **What did you think about before you tried the *handblasters?***

◆ **Did they feel like you thought they would? Why or why not?**

◆ **What are some things you were afraid of before you tried the *handblasters?***

◆ **How did your opinion of those things change after you tried them?**

Say: **Sometimes trying new things can be risky, but when we go ahead and try them, they turn out to be worth the risk. For example, some kids are terrified of riding roller coasters. But after they ride one, they love riding roller coasters for the rest of their lives. Today we're going to talk about serving God. ☞ We can serve God by doing good things for others. But sometimes it seems risky to do good for others. Let's explore that risk.**

LEARNING LAB

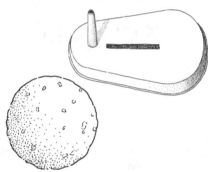

TEACHER TIP

It takes a couple of tries to get the hang of using the *handblasters*. Hold both *handblasters* in the palm of one hand. Toss one up and catch it against the other. There'll be a loud pop that sounds like a cap gun going off. The harder the *handblasters* strike together, the louder the pop will be. Don't worry! It doesn't hurt!

 THE **POINT**

LEARNING LAB

TEACHER TIP

Here's your chance to let your students' creativity show. Even though one item in the room might seem to be the totally logical choice to you, allow your students flexibility in their responses. As long as they can provide reasons for choosing the problem-solving object they pick, it's legitimate.

━━BIBLE INSIGHT

The words "prepared in advance" (Ephesians 2:10) refer to God's plan of events—specifically, to the circumstances of his people. God's purpose in the lives of people is seen in the way he creates situations allowing people the choice to obey or disobey as well as in God's direct ordering of people's circumstances. These divine activities are examples of God's providence.

QUEST!

(up to 15 minutes)

Say: **We're about to embark on a quest that will help us learn about the risk that is sometimes involved in doing good for others. Your instructions are on this *cassette tape.* Everything you need to fulfill your quest are your abilities and the Learning Lab items. Are you ready? Let's start!**

The point of the quest is for the kids to use the resources to help each other, so give them access to all the Learning Lab items. As it says on the *cassette tape,* the kids may only use a resource once to solve a problem and then it's "used up" for the rest of the quest.

Play the tape, and stop at appropriate points to allow the kids to decide how to solve each dilemma on the tape.

Collect and put away items from the Learning Lab as they're used in the quest so they don't get reused or distract the kids. After the quest, return all items to the Learning Lab.

When the quest is over, have kids form trios and take turns answering the following questions.

Ask:

◆ **What surprised you about the quest?**

◆ **How was going on this quest like real life?**

◆ **Was it easy or hard to figure out what resources to use to solve the various problems? Explain.**

◆ **Did you ever feel like you might not be able to do the quest? Why or why not?**

Say: **God has specific plans for you while you are here on earth. Some people look all their lives and never are able to see what God wants. Let's see if you can figure out what he wants. One key is found in Ephesians 2:10. Look the verse up and put it into your own words.**

Give kids paper and pencils, and give them a minute to look up the verse and reshape it into their own words. Then have volunteers share their versions with the class.

Ask:

◆ **According to this verse, how is God involved in your good works?**

◆ **How important do you think it is to God that we do good things for other people? Explain.**

◆ **What kinds of opportunities might we have to do good things for others?**

◆ **Can we create opportunities to do good things for others? Explain.**

Say: **We can serve God by doing good things for others. Our lives can be adventures as we see opportunities to do good things for others and figure out the best way to do them. God planned for his people to serve him by taking care of each other and other people they meet.**

**THE POINT**

THE RUB

(up to 12 minutes)

Have kids sit in a circle. Ask:

◆ **What are some ways that we can serve others?**

◆ **What's frightening or difficult about serving?**

Say: **There are all sorts of ways to do good things for others. Some of those things are intimidating and risky. For example, you could invite a homeless person to have dinner with your family. This may be a risky thing to do because you can't know if the homeless person is honest or trustworthy. But not all kinds of service are that risky. Doing good and serving can be accomplished simply in the way you interact with others. Let me show you what I mean.**

Hold up two *pumice rocks,* and say: **I'm going to pass these rocks around the circle. When a rock comes to you, I'd like you to hold it in each of your hands, rub your fingers against it, and then pass it on to the next person. After you've handled the rock, hold both of your hands out in front of you.**

Pass one rock around the circle in each direction. When the rocks return to you, say: **If you rub your hands and fingers together, you'll notice that the *pumice rock* rubbed off on you. It's the same way with serving others. The things you do rub off on those around you.**

Have kids form groups of three to discuss:

◆ **How have you seen others rub off on you in your own experiences?**

◆ **How have you rubbed off on someone else?**

◆ **How can you serve someone just in the way you rub off on him or her?**

Call the group back together. Read **Galatians 6:7-10** aloud and then say: **Everything we do has consequences. Even when we're just acting a little grumpy, our attitude rubs**

LEARNING LAB

TEACHER TIP

Encourage active participation as students report back by following up kids' answers with questions such as "What did you mean by that?" and "Can you tell me more?"

THE **POINT**

THE **POINT**

LEARNING LAB

TEACHER TIP

If you have more than fifteen kids in your class, form groups of five. Have each group choose one person to be the Server. Have the other four kids in each group sit around the sheet of paper.

off on others. We can serve God by doing good things for and acting kindly toward others. When we do good things for or just act in a respectful and kind way toward others, we build them up and serve God. In everything we do, we have a chance to either serve God and others or ignore them and tear them down.

Ask:

◆ What are some small ways to serve God by doing good things for others?

◆ How can you serve God and others in your relationships with friends? In your relationships with family members?

◆ In what ways do you need to change the way you rub off on others?

Collect the *pumice rocks* for future use.

I'LL BE YOUR SERVER TODAY

(up to 13 minutes)

Form groups of three. Give each group one sheet of blank paper to use as a "table" and four photocopies of the "Cafe Service" handout (p. 127). Have each group choose one person to be the Server, and have the other two kids sit at the table to be served.

In each group, have the kids choose two items from the handouts and ask their Servers for advice. Servers will listen to the situations shared with them by their "customers." Each server has thirty seconds to come up with a helpful suggestion for his or her customers. For example, one group may choose "Flunked a Math Test" with a side order of "Obnoxious Little Brother." The Server's advice might be "I'll help you study for the next math test, and let's take your brother to the park and spend some special time with him."

After the thirty seconds are up, use the *handblasters* to signal a move. When you pop the *handblasters,* everyone must move to a different table and take a seat. But they don't have to stay in the same three-person groups. The last person to arrive at each table becomes the new Server. Play until everyone has had a chance to be a Server.

Signal to get kids' attention. After the last round, return the *handblasters* to the Learning Lab. Have kids stay at their tables and discuss the following questions with the rest of their group members.

Ask:

◆ **When you served, how did you feel as you tried to quickly come up with a way to help out the people at your table?**

◆ **How did the rest of you feel about saying you needed help with something? Explain.**

Have kids look up **Luke 22:24-27.** Have a volunteer in each group read the verses aloud while the others follow along in their own Bibles. Then have them discuss the following questions.

Ask:

◆ **Why is the person who serves more important than those sitting at the table?**

◆ **Why do you think serving is so important to God?**

◆ **Does this passage change the way you feel about serving? Why or why not?**

Say: 👉 **We can serve God by doing good things for others. God planned for people to show others what it's like to be loved by him. We show God's love when we do good things for others. And we follow Jesus' example.**

⌐KEY VERSE
CONNECTION

"But seek first his kingdom and his righteousness, and all these things will be given to you as well" (Matthew 6:33).

Preadolescents are naturally self-absorbed. How they fit in with their peers is often of paramount importance. This Key Verse can help kids realize that "fitting in" with God should be what they strive toward. Then, as they grow in God's kingdom, they can serve him by caring for others.

🕊 THE **POINT**

TABLE TALK

Christian education extends beyond the classroom into the home. Photocopy the "Table Talk" handout (p. 128) for this week, and send it home with your kids. Encourage kids and parents to use the handout to spark meaningful discussion on this week's topic. Follow up next week by asking kids how their discussions with their families went.

CLOSING

PASS IT ON

(up to 12 minutes)

Have kids gather around you. Tell students about a time your whole day was ruined because of a small unkindness that was shown to you. Then tell students about a time your whole day went well just because of one good thing that was done for you.

LEARNING LAB

THE **POINT**

Hold the *clacker balls* in front of the students. Put the plastic balls on opposite sides of each other so that they make a parallel line. Say: **Doing good things for others works just like these *clacker balls*.** Twirl one of the balls around so that it hits the other. Do it quickly enough to make contact but slow enough for kids to see it. As you say the next statement, spin the *clacker balls* around faster and faster making sure that the two plastic balls make contact. Say: **Doing good things for others helps them do good things for other people, just as hitting this plastic ball sends it in motion. The more good we do for others, the more they can spread the good feeling around. It just takes one good action to get the whole thing going.**

Have kids stand in a line behind you. Keep the *clacker balls* spinning and say: **I'm going to do a good thing for the person behind me by telling him or her one thing I like about his or her personality. When I'm done, I'll hand the *clacker balls* off. He or she must try to keep the balls going and then tell the next person in line one unique and special thing about his or her personality. When you're finished, pass the *clacker balls* on. Try to keep them spinning.**

After each student has had a turn, ask:

◆ **What good things have you received that you can pass on to others?**

◆ **How are you going to 📖 serve God by doing good for others today? this week?**

Close in prayer, asking God to open up opportunities to serve.

★ CAFE SERVICE ★

Choose items from the menu, and ask your server for advice.

Small Problems

Broke a Shoelace
Can't Get Locker Open
Missed the Bus
Spilled Ketchup on Shirt
Flat Tire on Bike
Lost Lunch Money
Homework Gets Torn
Can't Get a Ride to the Mall

Home Problems

Parents Divorce
Obnoxious Little Brother
Grandparents Move In
Unfair Division of Chores
Big Fight With Dad

School Problems

Flunked Math Test
English Teacher Hates Me
Bully Stole Everything in My Locker
Lost a Library Book
Class Acts Up for Substitute Teacher

Friend Problems

Made Fun of by Popular Kids
Fight With Best Friend
A Friend Tells My Secret to Everybody
Not Invited to Biggest Party of the Year
Enemy Spreads Untrue Rumor About Me

Table Talk

Group's **hands-On BiBLE** curriculum™

Something to Think About

Chrissie McKenny began to learn sign language at church. During the services, she would participate in "expressive worship" where she would sign along with some of the songs.

One day, while driving past a school for the deaf, Chrissie asked her mom if they could stop in and see if there was anything she could help with. The school was hesitant at first because Chrissie was only eleven years old. But they made an exception. Every Thursday afternoon, Chrissie volunteers at the school. She helps other girls prepare for their evening activities and reads to them using sign language.

(taken from *Kid Heroes* by Neal Schusterman)

Sometimes opportunities for helping others just fall into our laps. Maybe your church provides important things for you to do to help out. But sometimes you may have to seek out the opportunities. It's always intimidating to get started. But after a few tries, you'll feel like a pro and you'll wonder why you were ever afraid to help out.

"Suppose a brother or sister is without clothes and daily food. If one of you says to him, 'Go, I wish you well; keep warm and well fed,' but does nothing about his physical needs, what good is it?"

(James 2:15-16)

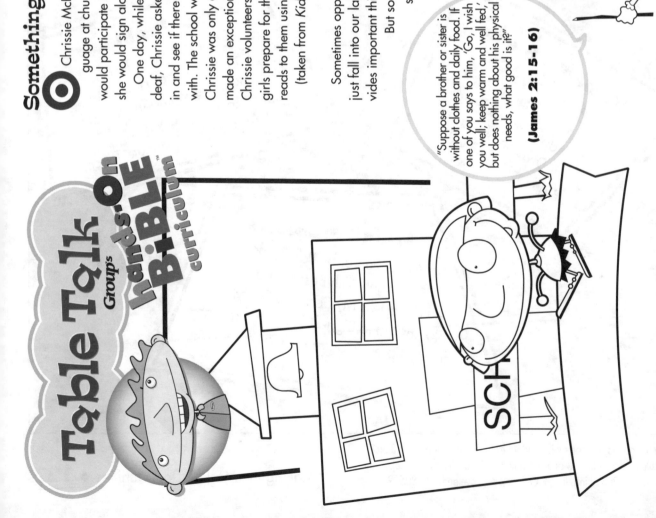

SCH...

Discussion Starters

● • Share an experience when you helped someone else.
  • What feelings surrounded the event?

Family Building

For Kids Only: Make a list of all the things others have done to help you. Include your parents, teachers, and church leaders on the list.

For Parents Only: Reach out to someone by meeting a need that an organization may not meet. For example, if a neighbor has plenty of money but seems a little lonely, ask him or her over for dinner.

For the Family: Have each family member choose a place he or she would like to go to volunteer or choose a place to go together as a family. Follow up on your commitment and begin helping others.

TIME FOR GOD

THE POINT

☞ **God wants us to set aside time to spend with him.**

THE BIBLE BASIS

Daniel 6:6-10

So the administrators and the satraps went as a group to the king and said: "O King Darius, live forever! The royal administrators, prefects, satraps, advisers and governors have all agreed that the king should issue an edict and enforce the decree that anyone who prays to any god or man during the next thirty days, except to you, O king, shall be thrown into the lions' den. Now, O king, issue the decree and put it in writing so that it cannot be altered—in accordance with the laws of the Medes and Persians, which cannot be repealed." So King Darius put the decree in writing.

Now when Daniel learned that the decree had been published, he went home to his upstairs room where the windows opened toward Jerusalem. Three times a day he got down on his knees and prayed, giving thanks to his God, just as he had done before.

KEY *VERSE*
for Lessons 10–13

"But seek first his kingdom and his righteousness, and all these things will be given to you as well."
(Matthew 6:33)

God gave Daniel wisdom. Daniel's governing skills were impressive—so impressive that Darius the Mede employed him when the Medes conquered Babylon, and even gave Daniel more responsibility. This made the other governors under Darius jealous, and they used Daniel's devotion to God against him. Fully aware of the consequences, Daniel still chose to spend time openly with God.

Today's young Christians don't face the life-or-death issue Daniel faced when they're considering how to spend time with God. They do, however, face the challenge of overcoming the idea that spending time with God is "inconvenient." We can help kids learn the importance of setting time aside to be alone with God.

This week's lesson explores biblical examples and encourages kids to consider the benefits of a healthy devotional life.

Other Scriptures used in this lesson are **Matthew 4:4; Luke 6:12-13;** and **Ephesians 5:15-16.**

GETTING THE POINT

Students will
◆ learn the value of time,
◆ discover why spending time with God may be difficult,
◆ examine how they spend their time, and
◆ talk about how they can include God in their schedules.

THIS LESSON AT A GLANCE

Before the lesson, collect the necessary items from the Learning Lab for the activities you plan to use. Refer to the pictures in the margin to see what each item looks like.

SECTION	MINUTES	WHAT STUDENTS WILL DO	LEARNING LAB SUPPLIES	CLASSROOM SUPPLIES
ATTENTION GRABBER	up to 10	**Measure of Time**—Guess how long it will take for an object to stop spinning.	Balancing eagle	Watch with a second hand
BIBLE EXPLORATION AND APPLICATION	up to 10	**Too Many Things!**—Create a distracting environment for volunteers trying to memorize Daniel 6:6-10 and explore Luke 6:12-13.	Balancing eagle, clacker balls, sticky sports ball, fiber optic flashlight	Bibles
	up to 15	**Bread Alone?**—Try to hear Matthew 4:4 being read over the sound of annoying noises and then discuss Daniel 6:6-10.	Whip whistle, cassette: "Noise"	Bibles, cassette player
	up to 15	**Rings of Time**—Determine how time is spent in an average day and discuss Ephesians 5:15-16.	Plastic rings	Bibles, "Rings of Time" handouts (p. 137), pencils
CLOSING	up to 5	**Ring Reminder**—Make a commitment to spending time with God.	Plastic rings	
QUARTER REVIEW	up to 5	**Reflection**—Review what they've learned over the past thirteen weeks.	All Learning Lab items	

Remember to make photocopies of the "Table Talk" handout (p. 138) to send home with your kids. "Table Talk" is a valuable tool for helping fifth- and sixth-graders talk with their parents about what they're learning in class.

THE LESSON

When kids arrive, remind them that you'll sound the *noisemaker* when you need their attention and you'll wait for all of them to look at you without talking before you continue.

Before you begin the lesson, ask kids about last week's "Table Talk" discussions. Use questions such as "How have you thought about people who have helped you?" and "How were you able to help others?" However, be careful not to alienate students whose families chose not to use "Table Talk."

ATTENTION GRABBER

MEASURE OF TIME

(up to 10 minutes)

Cover any clocks in the room, and have kids take off their watches. Place the *balancing eagle* on a table so that everyone can see it. Have a watch with a second hand ready so you can keep track of time.

Say: **We're going to see how good you are at guessing time. Watch closely and concentrate as I spin the *balancing eagle*. When it stops spinning, I will ask you how long you think it took for it to stop.**

Set the eagle on its stand, and give it a gentle spin. After the *balancing eagle* stops spinning, ask several students:

◆ **How long do you think it took for the *balancing eagle* to stop spinning?**

Reveal the actual time and then ask:

◆ **Did it feel like more time went by than the amount that actually did? Why or why not?**

◆ **Did you begin to feel bored after awhile? Explain.**

◆ **Do you ever feel bored when you spend time with God?**

◆ **Why does it seem like time moves slowly when you spend time with God?**

Say: **Time is a precious gift from God. We can never get time back once we've spent it.**  **God wants us to set aside time to spend with him. Today, we're going to take a look at how we spend our time and how we can make God a top priority.**

LEARNING LAB

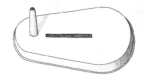

TEACHER TIP

Practice spinning the *balancing eagle* so that you can make it spin for approximately one minute.

THE **POINT**

LEARNING LAB

━BIBLE *INSIGHT*

When Daniel prayed in defiance of King Darius' decree, he went to the room where the windows faced Jerusalem. As Daniel prayed, he may have remembered the words of Solomon as he spoke about what could happen if the people of Israel were taken captive because of their disobedience. "And if they turn back to you with all their heart and soul in the land of their captivity where they were taken, and *pray toward the land* you gave their fathers, toward the city you have chosen and toward the temple I have built for your Name; then from heaven, your dwelling place, hear their prayer and their pleas, and uphold their cause" (2 Chronicles 6:38-39a).

BIBLE EXPLORATION AND APPLICATION

TOO MANY THINGS!

(up to 10 minutes)

Have kids form groups of no more than five. Ask for one volunteer from each group, and inform kids that you will rotate volunteers at one-minute intervals. Instruct volunteers to do one of the following tasks: spin the *balancing eagle;* play toss with the other members of their group using the *sticky sports ball;* keep the *clacker balls* going; or count the fibers on the *fiber optic flashlight.*

Say: **I'm going to read a Bible passage aloud. Everyone should try to memorize the passage as I read it. The volunteers should try to memorize the passage while completing the tasks assigned to them. When I say "Go," begin your tasks and I will begin reading. When I'm finished, I will ask you to repeat the passage back to me. Any questions?**

Say: **Go.** Read **Daniel 6:6-10** in a loud voice. Then, one at a time, have group members each attempt to recite the passage back to each other. Rotate volunteers and read the passage again. Keep rotating until each member of each group has had a turn as a volunteer. Collect the Learning Lab supplies, and ask:

◆ **What went through your mind as I was reading the passage?**

◆ **How do you think you might have remembered the passage better?**

◆ **What did you experience during this activity when you were not a volunteer?**

◆ **How was trying to memorize a Scripture passage while doing something else like trying to study while the television is going, your mom is talking, or the phone is ringing?**

◆ **What distractions do you face during your time with God?**

Say: **Time is a precious commodity. Let's turn to a passage that can tell us more.** Have someone in each group read **Luke 6:12-13** aloud as others follow along in their own Bibles. Ask groups to discuss the following questions:

◆ **What things in these verses make you think Jesus felt time with God was important?**

◆ **What things did Jesus do to make sure he didn't have a lot of distractions?**

◆ **What can we learn from what Jesus did?**

Encourage volunteers to share insights from their small-group discussions with the whole group.

Say: **Jesus clearly sets an example for us to follow. From this passage, we discover that** **God wants us to set aside time to spend with him.**

☜ THE **POINT**

BREAD ALONE?

(up to 15 minutes)

Direct kids to line up side by side facing a wall. Say: **I'm going to try to convey a message to you. Once you hear my message, I want you to act on it immediately.** Play the "Noises" segment on the *cassette tape* and quietly instruct kids to get their Bibles and read **Matthew 4:4.** Give kids your message in a whisper that they cannot hear while the *cassette tape* is playing.

Turn the *cassette tape* off, and ask kids if they heard your message. Say: **I'm going to give you the message again, this time using the *whip whistle*. When it's your turn, hold the *whip whistle* to your ear and listen for my message.** Turn the *cassette tape* back on, and convey your message by whispering it through the *whip whistle*. After kids have finished reading the passage, discuss the following questions:

◆ **Why couldn't you hear the message I had for you the first time I gave it?**

◆ **Were you able to hear the message when I spoke it through the *whip whistle*?**

◆ **What things make it difficult to hear God?**

◆ **What things make it easier for you to hear God's direction?**

◆ **How does the Bible make it easier for you to hear God?**

◆ **How is the *whip whistle* like the Bible? How is it different?**

Ask volunteers to read aloud **Daniel 6:6-10** as others follow along. Then have kids return to their groups from the previous activity and take turns answering the following questions. After each question, have volunteers summarize what they discussed for the whole group to hear. Ask:

◆ **What challenge did Daniel face?**

◆ **What similar challenges do you face in your time with God?**

LEARNING LAB

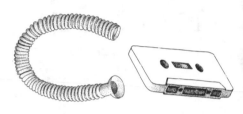

⎺KEY VERSE CONNECTION

"But seek first his kingdom and his righteousness, and all these things will be given to you as well" (Matthew 6:33).

Basketball practice. Homework. Youth group. Trips to the mall. When in your fifth- and sixth-graders' busy lives is there time for God? Use the Key Verse to emphasize that spending time with God is not just another item to fit into a hectic schedule—it's a priority set by God.

TEACHER TIP

Encourage active participation as students report back by following up kids' answers with questions such as "What did you mean by that?" and "Can you tell me more?"

◆ **If you had to make a similar choice, what choice do you think you'd make? Explain.**

◆ **What can you do to fight through the obstacles that make it difficult for you to hear God's direction?**

Say: **Sometimes we have to make conscious choices to spend time with people—even people we care about.** 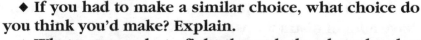 **God wants us to set aside time to spend with him, too. There are many distractions and obstacles that we have to work through to spend time with God. But he has given us the Bible and his promise to help us.**

THE **POINT**

LEARNING LAB

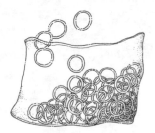

RINGS OF TIME

(up to 15 minutes)

Keep kids in the same groups of five. Give each group twenty-four *plastic rings,* a copy of the "Rings of Time" handout (p. 137), and a pencil. Say: **The rings I have given you each represent one hour. In your groups, I would like you to discuss how each hour of a typical fifth- or sixth-grader's day is spent. Place the rings in the boxes on your handout to represent each activity. For example, put eight rings in eight boxes for eight hours spent sleeping. Under the boxes, write the name of the activity.**

When kids are finished, have them take turns answering the following questions in their groups:

◆ **Did any of the groups have any rings left over? Did any use all their rings?**

◆ **For those of you who had rings left over, how can you spend your extra time with God?**

◆ **For those of you who used all of your rings, how can you rearrange your schedule so that you can make time for God?**

Say: **Let's look at Ephesians 5:15-16.**

Have a volunteer read aloud the passage for the whole group and then discuss the following questions:

◆ **What does this passage say about how we should spend our time?**

◆ **What does it mean to make the most of every opportunity?**

◆ **How then should we spend our free time?**

Say: **Sometimes it's hard to place a value on time. It seems as though there will always be more and more of it.**  **God wants us to set aside time to spend with him. And he promises that the time we spend with him will be worth the effort. Let's make a personal commitment to spend time with God regularly.**

TEACHER TIP

It's important to say The Point just as it's written in each activity. Repeating The Point over and over throughout the lesson will help kids remember it and apply it to their lives.

THE **POINT**

TABLE TALK

Christian education extends beyond the classroom into the home. Photocopy the "Table Talk" handout (p. 138) for this week, and send it home with your kids. Encourage kids and parents to use the handout to spark meaningful discussion on this week's topic. Follow up next week by asking kids how their discussions with their families went.

CLOSING

RING REMINDER

(up to 5 minutes)

Have kids spread out around the room and sit on the floor. Spread out the *plastic rings* on the table. Say: **I would like you to make a personal commitment to making time for God. You can come up and take a ring as a reminder of your commitment. Each ring represents ten minutes. Take the number of rings that represent your daily commitment. For example, if you take three rings, you are committing to spend thirty minutes a day with God. God is more precious than any thing in this world. He created us to have relationship with him.** ☞ **God wants us to set aside time to spend with him.**

LEARNING LAB

☜ THE **POINT**

QUARTER REVIEW

REFLECTION

(up to 5 minutes)

Form a circle, and pass the Learning Lab box with all the Learning Lab items in it around the circle. Have everyone choose one item out of the box that reminds them of something they've learned over the past quarter.

Next, have kids form pairs. Have partners take turns telling each other why they chose the items they did and what experiences from the past thirteen lessons their items remind

LEARNING LAB

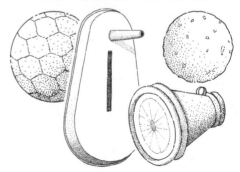

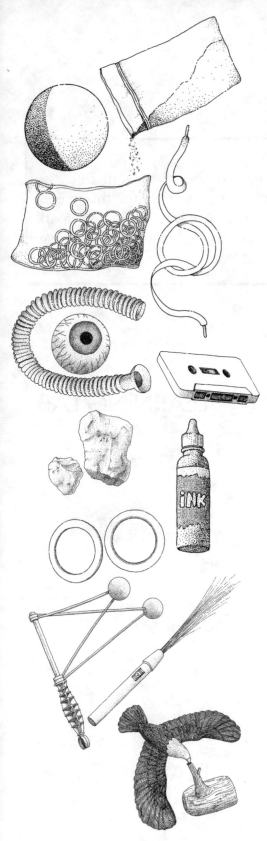

them of. Then have pairs join together to form groups of no more than four. In their foursomes, have kids take turns completing these sentences:

◆ "The Learning Lab item I chose helped me learn…"

◆ "One Scripture from the past class sessions that's encouraged me is…"

◆ "One thing I'll do differently because of something I learned in this class is…"

Dismiss with a prayer of thanks for what your kids have learned through this course.

Rings of Time

Table Talk

Group's **hands-On BiBLE** curriculum

Discussion Starter

◎ ◆ What things in your life steal away your time with God?

Family Building

*For Kids Only: Make a commitment to have a daily devotion or quiet time. Every day, have your time with God at the same location during the same time of day. Start by just spending ten minutes each day. If you find you need more time, start taking it.

*For Parents Only: If you're struggling in your devotions, go to a Christian bookstore and ask the salesperson to help you find a dynamic and helpful devotion book to use.

*For the Family: Create a holiday in your family by having a one-hour quiet time. Have everyone in your family go to a quiet place with a Bible to pray. Set a timer for one hour. Don't worry if some family members fall asleep. Just make sure to spend awake times with God. After the timer rings, cook a family feast together to celebrate your relationship with God. Mark this day on your calendar every year.

◎

Something to Think About

◎ ◆ 57 percent of adolescents say they spent time reading yesterday.

◆ 48 percent of thirteen- to fifteen-year-olds say they read the paper daily.

◆ At least 92 percent of adolescents say they listened to the radio yesterday.

◆ On average, kids aged six to eleven watch over twenty-one hours of television a week.

◆ 80 percent of high school sophomores say they talk to friends on the telephone at least once or twice a week.

(taken from *Statistical Handbook on Adolescents in America* by Bruce A. Chadwick and Tim B. Heaton)

How much time do you spend doing all those things? How much time do you spend with God every day? There are so many things in life that quietly and slowly steal away all of our time. We all want to work on our relationships with God. We all want to grow closer to him and to know him more. But somehow, time slips away and we miss the opportunity. Don't let it happen tomorrow. Plan to spend time with God, to read the Bible, and to pray. Don't let all the distractions of this world steal away your relationship with God.

"In the morning, O Lord, you hear my voice; in the morning I lay my requests before you and wait in expectation" **(Psalm 5:3).**

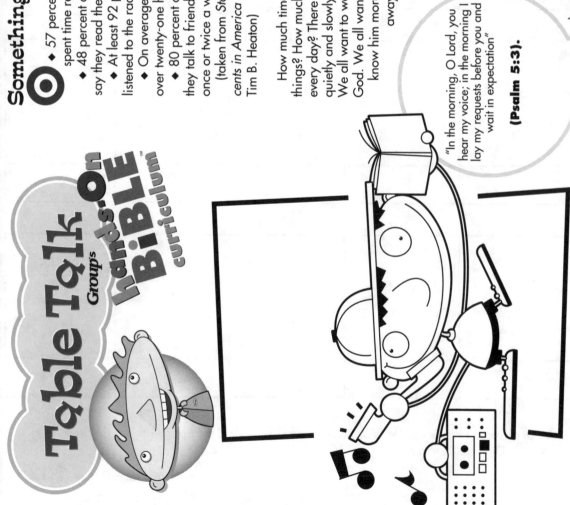

Time for God, Week 13

Permission to photocopy this handout from Group's Hands-On Bible Curriculum™ for Grades 5 and 6 granted for local church use. Copyright © Group Publishing, Inc., P.O. Box 481, Loveland, CO 80539.

BONUS IDEAS

GREAT GAMES

Acting Up—Have the kids form a circle. Ask for one student to approach you and listen into the *whip whistle* as you whisper the name of a character from the Christmas story. Then have the student stand in the middle of the circle and silently pantomime the character. Have the rest of the class guess which character is being acted out. Give each student a different character from the Christmas story so the class can act out the whole story at the end.

Swinging-Rings Relay—Tie a *bottle ring* to each end of two *neon shoelaces*. Have kids form two teams, and have them line up single file at one end of the room. Set the two *prism scopes* on the floor at the other end of the room.

Give each team one of the shoelaces with the rings on the ends. On "go," have the first person in each line hook one of the rings over one ear and run to his or her team's *prism scope*. Without touching the shoelace, he or she must get the ring on the end of the shoelace to fall flat on the floor over the *prism scope*. When the first person is successful, he or she will run back to the team and give the shoelace to the next person, who then repeats the action. The first team to have all team members finish wins.

This game works well with the lessons on relationships.

Circuit Relay—Form five teams. Each team must have at least two people. Set up five stations around the room with the Learning Lab items and explain them to the kids.

Station 1: Kids toss the *handblasters* back and forth and make them blast. Each blast is worth one point.

Station 2: Kids bounce the *two-tone superball* back and forth. Each caught bounce is worth one point.

Station 3: Kids fit small *plastic rings* onto a *neon shoelace* one at a time. Each strung *plastic ring* is worth one point.

Station 4: Kids toss the *sticky sports ball* back and forth. Each time a player catches the ball, it counts as one point.

Station 5: Kids stand three feet away from the *prism scope* and toss the *bottle rings* at it. A point is scored each time a *bottle ring* "rings" the *prism scope*.

Assign each team to one of the stations. Give teams each a pencil and a sheet of paper to keep track of their score for each station. On "go," teams each will have twenty seconds to do their activity. After twenty seconds are up, sound time with a *noisemaker*. Remind teams to write down their scores and then have each team rotate to the next station. Continue until each team has been to each station. The team with the highest score wins.

AFFIRMATION ACTIVITIES

"I Have a Secret"—Have kids sit in a circle. Use the *whip whistle* to whisper a positive comment about someone in class to the person sitting next to you. Then give the *whip whistle* to the person sitting next to you and have him or her whisper the same comment to the next person in the circle. Continue until the affirmation has gone all the way around the circle. Play a round for each student sitting in the circle.

On the Ball—Give everyone a ballpoint pen. Have kids stand in a circle. Tell about something positive that someone in the group has done for someone else. As you talk, use a ballpoint pen to write that person's name or initials in tiny letters on the *two-tone superball,* but don't tell the person's name. Then bounce the ball to the person. That person then does the same for someone else. No one can get the ball twice. Keep going until everyone's name is on the ball. Then say, "Our whole class is really on the ball!"

Time Is Short—Have kids form pairs. Give partners a minute to complete this sentence for each other: "If I had one hour to spend with you this week, I'd want to do this for you: _____." Students might say "help you with your homework" or "take you on a bike ride." Then use a *noisemaker* to signal time to change partners. Each time partners change, the time they have to do something nice is cut. Use these times: one hour, one-half hour, fifteen minutes, five minutes, and one minute.

Something for You—Write each person's name on a separate slip of paper, and put the slip in a bowl or bag. Have kids each draw out a name; that person will be their secret partner. Give each student a catalog or a newspaper advertising-supplement, a sheet of paper, and a pencil. Give kids three minutes to come up with lists of things they'd like to buy for their partners. They each have $5,000 to spend. Then have them share their lists with their partners. This works well with the lessons on relationships.

To make this activity work with the money and time module, have kids brainstorm gifts they'd give to homeless people. Or stage a competition in which each student thinks of a thoughtful gift for the least amount of money.

PARTIES AND PROJECTS

"Jesus' Birthday Party!"—Before the party, have kids select a mission to support such as a food bank, a homeless shelter, a needy family, or a missionary. Have the kids bring small gifts that can be donated to the mission.

Decorate the room with balloons, streamers, and confetti. Play praise or Christmas music. Play party games and then let students each place their gift in front of a picture of Jesus and say, "Thank you for coming to earth for me." Conclude the party with a birthday cake and an energetic rendition of "Happy Birthday to You" sung to Jesus.

Relationship Tunes—Have kids bring in their favorite songs about relationships. The music can be about romance, friendship, or any other kind of relationship. Play all of the songs and discuss the viewpoints and values represented in the music. Compare the relationships described in the songs with the principles you've been studying from the Bible.

Togetherness Getaway—Have a one-night retreat or lock-in that emphasizes building relationships. Some ideas to try:

◆ Have kids create name tags that describe who they are. For example, someone who loves the water might make a name tag in the shape of a boat.

◆ Form trios and tie kids together at the wrists for a couple of hours. Have trio members learn everything they can about each other during those two hours.

◆ Set up a "bean-based" scoring system. Give a bean every time someone uses the word "you" in a sentence, and take away a bean every time someone uses "I" or "me."

♦ Play games such as softball, basketball, soccer, volleyball, Tag or just about any other active game. Have kids pair up and have partners hold hands through the whole game.

♦ Have teams of three be responsible for all major duties: setup, meal preparation, cleanup, and any other chores. Make sure they work together and get to know each other in the process.

Budget Party—Set a budget of $50 for kids to spend on a party, and let the kids do all the planning. Encourage kids to plan for food, invitations, decorations, games, and prizes. Help kids organize their priorities if they ask for help. Remind kids to be flexible so they don't get too discouraged if their taste exceeds their budget.

Take the kids shopping to see how well their plans fit their budget. Help them make adjustments to the plan in order to stick to the budget.

Then have kids invite their friends and throw a great party!

Say It and Do It!—Have kids brainstorm ways to serve the church and the community. Write down everyone's ideas. Have kids vote on the service project they want to do first. Work with kids to plan the service project as soon as possible. After the event, have kids tell what they learned from serving others.

Refer to the list of service ideas often, and have kids choose other projects to do. You might want to plan a service project every month.

HOBC Marketing Survey

Please help Group Publishing continue to provide innovative and exciting resources to help your children know, love, and follow Christ. Take a moment to fill out and send back this survey. Thanks!

1. What level(s) of Hands-On Bible Curriculum™ are you using?

2. How many children are in your class? adult helpers?

3. How has the size of your class changed since using Hands-On Bible Curriculum?

❑ Remained the same   ❑ Grown a lot
❑ Grown a little   ❑ Other _____

Comments

4. When do you use Hands-On Bible Curriculum?

❑ Sunday school   ❑ Midweek group
❑ Children's church   ❑ Other (please describe) _____
_____
_____

5. What do you like best about the curriculum?

6. Is there anything about the curriculum you would like to see changed? (For example, if a certain lesson didn't work well, what specific changes would you recommend?)

7. What products would you like to see Group Publishing develop to fill specific needs in your church?

BRING THE BIBLE TO LIFE FOR YOUR 1ST- THROUGH 6TH-GRADERS... WITH GROUP'S HANDS-ON BIBLE CURRICULUM™

Energize your kids with Active Learning!

Group's **Hands-On Bible Curriculum**™ will help you teach the Bible in a radical new way. It's based on Active Learning—the same teaching method Jesus used.

In each lesson, students will participate in exciting and memorable learning experiences using fascinating gadgets and gizmos you've not seen with any other curriculum. Your elementary students will discover biblical truths and <u>remember</u> what they learn because they're <u>doing</u> instead of just listening.

You'll save time and money, too!

While students are learning more, you'll be working less—simply follow the quick and easy instructions in the **Teacher Guide**. You'll get tons of material for an energy-packed 35- to 60-minute lesson. And, if you have extra time, there's an arsenal of Bonus Ideas and Time Stuffers to keep kids occupied—and learning! Plus, you'll SAVE BIG over other curriculum programs that require you to buy expensive separate student books—all student handouts in Group's **Hands-On Bible Curriculum** are photocopiable!

In addition to the easy-to-use **Teacher Guide**, you'll get all the essential teaching materials you need in a ready-to-use **Learning Lab**®. No more running from store to store hunting for lesson materials—all the active-learning tools you need to teach 13 exciting Bible lessons to any size class are provided for you in the **Learning Lab**.

Challenging topics each quarter keep your kids coming back!

Group's **Hands-On Bible Curriculum** covers topics that matter to your kids and teaches them the Bible with integrity. Switching topics every month keeps your 1st- through 6th-graders enthused and coming back for more. The full two-year program will help your kids...

- make God-pleasing decisions,
- recognize their God-given potential, and
- seek to grow as Christians.

Take the boredom out of Sunday school, children's church, and midweek meetings for your elementary students. Make your job easier and more rewarding with no-fail lessons that are ready in a flash. Order Group's **Hands-On Bible Curriculum** for your 1st- through 6th-graders today.

Hands-On Bible Curriculum is also available for Toddlers & 2s, Preschool, and Pre-K and K!